Young Writers
2004 POETRY COMPETITION

ONCE UPON A RHYME

IMAGINATION FOR
A NEW GENERATION

Scottish Regions Vol II
Edited by Donna Samworth

 Young**Writers**

First published in Great Britain in 2005 by:
Young Writers
Remus House
Coltsfoot Drive
Peterborough
PE2 9JX
Telephone: 01733 890066
Website: www.youngwriters.co.uk

SB ISBN 1 84460 648 1

Foreword

Young Writers was established in 1991 and has been passionately devoted to the promotion of reading and writing in children and young adults ever since. The quest continues today. Young Writers remains as committed to engendering the fostering of burgeoning poetic and literary talent as ever.

This year's Young Writers competition has proven as vibrant and dynamic as ever and we are delighted to present a showcase of the best poetry from across the UK. Each poem has been carefully selected from a wealth of *Once Upon A Rhyme* entries before ultimately being published in this, our twelfth primary school poetry series.

Once again, we have been supremely impressed by the overall high quality of the entries we have received. The imagination, energy and creativity which has gone into each young writer's entry made choosing the best poems a challenging and often difficult but ultimately hugely rewarding task - the general high standard of the work submitted amply vindicating this opportunity to bring their poetry to a larger appreciative audience.

We sincerely hope you are pleased with our final selection and that you will enjoy *Once Upon A Rhyme Scottish Regions Vol II* for many years to come.

Contents

Adam Hamilton (11)	14
Craig Smith (9)	14
Eilidh McCulloch (8)	15
Findlay Strain (8)	15
Gavin Wilkie (8)	15
Hannah Jakobsen (8)	16
Kalum Turnbull (8)	16
Tilly Hepburn-Wright (9)	16
Victoria Laidlaw (8)	17
Alreis Fairbairn (10)	17
Amie Stewart (9)	17
Andrew Fyfe (9)	18
Ashleigh Macarthur (10)	18
Brodie Walker (9)	18
Jacquelyn Wilson (9)	19
Lesley Forbes (9)	19
Mhairi Docherty (9)	19
Lynne Macarthur (9)	20
Rhiannon Morrison (9)	20
Simon MacDonald (9)	21
Shanice MacLennan (10)	21
Michael Ashmole (10)	22
George MacIntosh (10)	22
Charlotte MacKintosh	23
Billy Aitken (11)	23
Emma Mackintosh (11)	24
Samantha Birkbeck (10)	24
Niall McCulloch (9)	25
Danielle Murray (11)	25
Angus Paterson (9)	26
Kate Paterson (11)	27
Sophie Strain (11)	27
Lauren Urquhart (10)	28
Toni Wilson (11)	29
Eilidh Montgomery (10)	30

Conon Primary School, Dingwall

Gordon Urquhart (7)	30
Ethan Bushell (7)	30
Jordan Garden (7)	31
Kieran McSwegan	31

Corstorphine Primary School, Edinburgh

Yvette Rosie (10)	50
Jordan McKay (9)	50
Scott Edmond (10)	51
Robbie Taylor (10)	51
Selina McPherson (10)	52
Caitlin Snell (9)	52
Claire Paxton (10)	53
David Provan (10)	53
Hannah McCall (10)	54
Steven Leahey (10)	54
Stephanie McKenzie (9)	55
Hannah Marshall (9)	55
Ellie Blair (9)	56
Natasha Wyllie (10)	57
Reem Ryanne (9)	58
Beth Mooney (9)	58

Craigbank Primary School, Larkhall

Isabell Lee (10)	59
Graham Rock (10)	59
Robbie Wells (10)	60
Shereen McEwan (10)	60
William Marshall Miller (11)	61
Craig Williams (10)	61
David Marshall (10)	62
Marc McGinty (9)	62
Charles Brady (9)	63
David Lyden (9)	63
Damien McQueen (10)	64
Andrew Mayberry (9)	64
Christopher Cole (9)	65
Kane Bennett (9)	65
Jordan Hollands (9)	66

Falla Hill Primary School, Fauldhouse

Karen Taylor (11)	66
Laura Dodds (11)	67
Leigh Salmond (11)	68
Jordan Kelly (11)	68
Stephanie Roden (11)	69
Abby McKay (11)	69

Derek Smith (11)   70
Jordan McDonald (11)   70
Emma Merrilees (11)   71
Laura Swan (11)   71
Colene Copland (11)   72
Ellie Lamont (10)   72
Ashley Smillie (10)   73

Flora Stevenson Primary School, Edinburgh
Cara Targett-Ness (7)   73
Aaron Heinemeier (7)   73
Anna Hale (8)   74
Duncan Player (8)   74
Nadia Unis (8)   74
Ye Ye Xu (9)   75
Mark Jarvis (7)   75
Ella Duffy (7)   76
Varshini Vijayakumur (7)   76
Rebecca Morton (8)   77
Jenny Docherty (8)   77
Hannah Watson (10)   77
Caitlin Lewis (9)   78
Lily Roberts Thomson (9)   79
Aidan Targett-Ness (9)   79
Paul Oglesby (10)   80
Lauren Anderson (9)   80
Nicole Calder (10)   81
Katie Brown (9)   81
Chiara Crawford (8)   82

Granton Primary School, Edinburgh
Michael Venters (10)   82
Alexzandra Morrison (11)   83
Billy Robertson (9)   83
Michael Hutton (10)   84

Holy Family RC Primary School, Winchburgh
Ashleigh Gorman (8)   84
Garry Paterson (9)   85
Rebecca Telfer (8)   85

Ben Gallagher (8)	85
Laura Simpson (9)	86
Iona O'Hanlon	86
Sean Finnigan (8)	86
Caitlan Philbin (7)	87
Ciaran Reddington (7)	87
Shauna Green (6)	87
Megan Dalton (6)	88
Matthew Stirling (6)	88
Jessica Rooney (7)	88
Ryan Green (10)	89
Sarah Howard (10)	89
Connor Sinnet (10)	89
Declan Rennie (11)	90
Ryan Buchanan (10)	90
Connor Gallagher (11)	90
Yasmin Buchanan (10)	91
Ruairidh Gauld (11)	91
Jamie Griffiths (9)	91
Blair O'Hanlon (10)	92
Caitlin Rose Coyle (10)	92
Calum Telfer (9)	92
Jillian Angelique C Marin (10)	93
Marina McLean (10)	93
Natalia Donnelly-Kay (9)	93

Knightsridge Primary School, Livingston

Adam Mullen (9)	94
Connor Salmond (9)	94
Shannon Hagan (10)	94
Andrew Wishart (9)	95
Ryan Egan (10)	95
Alexander Rowland (8)	95
Jordan Troup (10)	96
Jordan Laing (10)	96
Darryl Beveridge (9)	97
Shawn Oliver Wright (9)	97
Dale Kennedy (8)	97

Lamington Primary School, Biggar

Andrew Komar (9)	98
Craig Gibson (9)	98
Stephen McKnight (11)	98
Ruth Bowman (9)	99
Richard Crosby (9)	99
Emma Craig (11)	99
Daisy Fox (9)	100
Claire Pilpel (11)	100
Lewis Loening (11)	100
Struan Collin (11)	101
Elizabeth McLatchie (11)	101
Kieran French (11)	102
Ellie McGill (11)	102
Cameron Murdoch (8)	103
Tara Jackson (10)	103
Callum Cross	103

Maryculter Primary School, Aberdeen

Rachel Green (9)	104
Robyn Martin (10)	104
Emma Anderson (11)	105
Philip Green (10)	105
Jamie Graham Pryde (9)	106
Calum Reddish (11)	106
Cameron Porter (7)	106
Abby Martin (8)	107
Matthew Davidson (11)	107
Scott Gammie (10)	108
Callum Boxall (9)	108
Connor Flewker-Barker (9)	109
Diderik Van Loon (9)	109
Carmen Gammie (7)	110
Kirsten Pryde (7)	110
Isabel Van Loon (7)	110
Sarah-Ann Stewart (7)	111
Kirby Brown (7)	111
Fiona Sutherland (8)	112

Muirtown Primary School, Inverness

Prestonfield Primary School, Edinburgh

Rosewell Primary School, Rosewell

Dale Elder (10)	149
Jade Ramsay (9)	149
Euan Hamilton (11)	150
Conner McConnell (11)	150
Brian Turnbull (10)	151
Joshua Blair (11)	151
Stuart Easton (10)	151

St Aidan's Primary School, Wishaw

Victoria Somerville (9)	152
Julie Dobbin (10)	152
Gemma Buick (11)	153
Lauren Smith (9)	153
Daniela Clare (9)	154
Maria Hainey	154
Aidan Dobbin (10)	154
Michael Carroll (10)	155
Ryan McCready (10)	155
Clare Pearson (11)	156
Amy Cassidy (9)	156
Emma Hay (11)	157
Nicolas Friskey (11)	157
Sophie McGinness (11)	158
Francesca Campbell (10)	158
Christopher McKeown (10)	159
Joseph Miller (10)	159
Kyle Neilly (10)	160
Jennifer Dyer (10)	160
Caitlin Foley (11)	161
Michael Donnelly (11)	161
Daniel Gaffney (11)	162
Darren Dobbin (11)	162
Andrew McCluskey (10)	162
Josh McPhail (10)	162
Cara McQuade (9)	163
Paul McCafferty (9)	163
Chloe Archer (9)	164
Katrina Mitchell (9)	164
Joseph Devine (10)	165
Emma McAlinden (10)	165

Alexander Smith (10)   179
Drew Anderson (11)   179
Megan Forde (11)   180
Romane Allanson (11)   180
Michael Faulkner (11)   181
Jamie Collier (11)   181
Alice Dalkin (10)   182
Joel Paatelainen (11)   182
Rhian Hughes (10)   183
Calum Fergusson (11)   183
Horace Li (10)   184
Stuart Noble (11)   184
Min Ke (11)   185
Andrew Mackay (11)   185
Fiona Armstrong (10)   186
Leila Marshall (10)   186
Eleanor Williams (10)   187
Kirsty Melton (11)   188
Annie Nicoll Baines (10)   189
Susie Purvis (11)   190
Kirsti Clark (10)   190
Jamie Long (11)   191

Springfield Primary School, Linlithgow

Eleanor Chadwick (10)   191
Conor Cochrane (11)   192
Clair Kirkwood (11)   192
Jamie Morrison (11)   192
Jed Anderson (11)   193
Sophie Lynch (11)   193
David Silk (11)   193
Joanna Graham (11)   194
Joanne Riddell (10)   194
Leah Swan (11)   194
Gareth Oliver (10)   195
Katie Allison (11)   195
Liam Ostlere (11)   195
Fiona McLean (11)   196
Kirsten Hall (10)   196
Callum Henry (10)   196
Karine Stalker (11)   197

Grant Andrew Maclean (11)	197
Corrie Hyslop (11)	197
Graeme Poole (11)	198
Sarah McDonald (11)	198
Allison Macdonald (11)	198
Lucy Pilcher (11)	199
Eilidh McCall (10)	199
Catriona Haig (10)	199
Neil Scullion (11)	200
Michael Boyle (11)	200
Rebecca Aitken (11)	200
Callum Alexander Small (11)	201
Shona Lawson (11)	201
Adam Sorbie (11)	201
Nicola Riddell (10)	202
Lesley Wilson (11)	202
Conall Black (11)	202
Chloé Milligan (10)	203
Douglas Watt (10)	203
David Joseph McKay (10)	203
Simrat Panesar (11)	204
Clare Gillies (11)	204
Lorn Henderson (10)	204
Kim-Louise McGregor (10)	205
Melissa Black (11)	205
James Mair (10)	205
Jamie Coyle (11)	206
Jill Stanners (11)	206
Neil Morrison (11)	206
Monique Elizabeth Yntema (10)	207
Campbell Thomson (11)	207
Julia Herd (11)	207
Robyn Brown (11)	208
Sam Parlett (11)	208
Emma Whitehead (11)	208
Mahri Nicholson (10)	209
Allyn Preece (10)	209
Lucy Nisbet (11)	209
Rebecca Sorrie (10)	210

Strathburn School, Inverurie

Craig Smith (10)	210
David Robertson (10)	211
Ross Napier (10)	211
Niomi Murison (10)	211
Dean Morris (9)	212
Molly Munro (10)	212
Katie Mackenzie (10)	213
Alice Rose McInulty (9)	213
Stefan Innes (9)	213
Lauren Gray (10)	214
Emily Florence (10)	214
Callum Drysdale (10)	214
Grant Dryburgh (10)	215
Emma Donaldson (9)	215
Rory Angus (10)	215
Nicole Aitken (10)	216

Stratherrick Primary School, Inverness

Hannah Slater (10)	216
Craig Hepburn (9)	216
Eleanor Parrott (10)	217
Lucy Fraser (10)	217
Iseabail Parrott (7)	218
Hannah Tweedlie (9)	218
Ruairidh Fraser (11)	218
Emma Fraser (8)	219
Kyle Easter (11)	219
Matthew Ricketts (9)	220
Fraser MacLennan (11)	220
Harry Stoppard (11)	221
Jak Bryant (10)	221
Annie Butterworth (10)	221
Melissa Cumming (7)	222
Ewen Fraser (9)	222

Townhead Primary School, Coatbridge

Jack Harrison (9)	223
Joseph Brannigan (10)	223
Mark Plunkett (9)	224

The Poems

Will You Play With Me?

Twinkle the rabbit was short and plump,
She liked to play with her friends by the big tree stump.
And on a fine morning the birds got up early
To tell Twinkle it was a new day,
So off she went to play.

'May I play with you baby goose?'
'No, no Twinkle I'm having a bath.'
'So,' said baby goose, 'don't disturb me,
Please go away, I don't want to play.'

Walking sadly from the pond,
She made her way to the hill beyond,
For in her mind she pictured quick,
A good friend with a walking stick,
It's Grandmum, she is old and kind,
But the day would soon be left behind,
She had to hurry to her home,
And was pleased to find she was alone!
But too old and tired to play -
So Twinkle went back home in dismay.

Her mum said, 'Watch out, she'll be here soon.'
'Who?' asked Twinkle. 'Who do you mean?'
'Your friend who's come to play, it's Jean.'

Florence Blackbourn (8)
Blackness Primary School, Linlithgow

The Problem With Pets

The problem with pets is very simple,
They can be as irritating as a pimple,
Or as soft as a cuddle.

It is not a good idea to keep two cats in your house,
They'd make a mess but would catch a mouse.
A gorilla would keep me warm at night,
But I would like one that didn't fight.

A unicorn would share ice cream,
A bird would help me fly so high.
A fish would help me learn to swim,
Although it would certainly concern him.

An elephant would give me a shower,
It would give me great trunk power,
But there is still a problem with pets.
A tiger and a deer would not get on,
They would fight until they were gone.

I've told you why pets can be bad,
But I just hope you will be glad,
To hear that pets can also be great,
They can be sweet and cute
And even live on the Isle of Bute!

Pets come in all shapes and sizes,
Some even come as prizes,
One thing I learn from week to week,
Is that all pets are simply unique.

Hannah Westwater (10)
Blackness Primary School, Linlithgow

A Load Of Nonsense

If pigs can fly,
Then why can't I?
Why aren't dragons soft and hairy?
Would scaly rabbits be quite scary?

The kangaroo would dare to jump,
But the elephant jumped up and down with a thump!
The tiger is the cuddliest of all beasts,
While the cat has the biggest of feasts.

Monkeys run the human race
And extraterrestrial too,
But if life was a load of nonsense,
It would be a zoo.

Danielle Fraser (10)
Blackness Primary School, Linlithgow

My Horse Of A Dog

My dog is a really jumpy dog,
She tosses her head and clears a log,
She gallops and trots around the park,
Just like the wind until it is dark.

If she smells chicken,
She bounds to the kitchen,
With head in the bin,
She'll make such a din.

She'll gallop around the wood like mad,
She nearly pulls the arms off Dad,
My dog is a nice horse after all,
If you meet her you'll have a ball.

Amy Cullen (9)
Blackness Primary School, Linlithgow

Daytime

Listen to the breeze rustling the leaves on the trees,
Birds singing songs all morning long.
All the children skipping in through the school gate,
Mums and dads so glad they are not late!
Playtime for all so outside we go,
Basketball, tennis, running and football,
Chatting with friends, someone has scored a goal!

Do you hear the bell ring?
It's time to line up and in we go,
Maths, English, German and handwriting to do.
Ten past twelve, tidy up time and over we go for lunch,
Food and drinks, there is always plenty to munch!
One o'clock everyone in and sitting down,
Everything's done and ready for art.
Teacher says we are going to be painting an ark!
Five to three and I've hurt my knee.
Three o'clock, home time, our faces fill with sorrow.
'Good afternoon all, I will see you all tomorrow!'

Kate McKerrow (11)
Blackness Primary School, Linlithgow

Kangaroo - Haiku

Bouncing kangaroo,
Golden-brown, fierce, stone kicking,
Boxing in the ring.

Nicholas Gunn (9)
Burghead Primary School, Elgin

Cat - Haiku

Big, wild furry cat,
Leaping high in the black sky,
Waiting still for mice.

Astrid Fares (8)
Burghead Primary School, Elgin

Unicorn - Haiku

Graceful unicorn,
Cantering around the field,
Showing who's the boss.

Beth Williamson (9)
Burghead Primary School, Elgin

Colourful Parrot - Haiku

Colourful parrot
Wakes me up with whistling
Silly, funny bird.

Darren Sim (9)
Burghead Primary School, Elgin

Panda - Haiku

Bamboo grass is green,
Panda bear has a white face,
Eating with his friends.

Alan Murray (8)
Burghead Primary School, Elgin

Foal - Haiku

Powerful, smooth foal,
Galloping brown and sparkling,
Peacefully sleeping.

Cara Phillips (9)
Burghead Primary School, Elgin

Frog - Haiku

Blue feet and slimy,
Brightly coloured means danger,
Black eyes looking round.

Heidi Christison (9)
Burghead Primary School, Elgin

Whale

Slowing moving blue whale,
100 tonnes of blue whale,
Favourite meal is krill.

Thomas Strike (9)
Burghead Primary School, Elgin

Eagle - Haiku

Swooping up and down,
Eating a tiny rabbit,
Swallowing it whole.

Angus Gordon (8)
Burghead Primary School, Elgin

Humpback Whale - Haiku

Humpback whale gets caught,
Tries to break free but he fails,
Goodbye humpback whale.

Scott Smith (9)
Burghead Primary School, Elgin

Otter - Haiku

Otter being wise,
He catches his prey quickly,
He is waterproof.

James Thomson (9)
Burghead Primary School, Elgin

Dragon - Haiku

Dragon red and green,
Fire fighter is nice and kind,
Fighting bad people.

Kieran Shand (9)
Burghead Primary School, Elgin

Dragon - Haiku

Nice and very kind,
Hungered dragon blowing fire,
At nasty people.

Bradley Philip (9)
Burghead Primary School, Elgin

Bunny - Haiku

Beautiful bunny,
Hopping around all day long,
Hops to its burrow.

Tanya McKenzie (9)
Burghead Primary School, Elgin

Recipe For Autumn

Take frosty, sunny mornings,
Raindrops as small as pinheads,
Then dull, damp evenings.

Add squirrels collecting nuts for winter,
Leaves falling swiftly from the trees,
Mice collecting too, but can't find any cheese!

And you have made autumn!

James Hitchmough (8)
Cawdor Primary School, Nairn

Recipe For Autumn

Take blustery wind blowing over the sea,
Blue rain falling from the sky,
Sparkling, white, freezing cold frost melting in my hands.

Add leaves as bright as the sun,
Leaves turning into different colours,
Leaves falling from the sky as soft as snow.

And you have made autumn.

Kyle Smith (7)
Cawdor Primary School, Nairn

Recipe For Autumn

Take bright cold mornings,
Frost like glittery stars.

Add leaves as brown as mud
Falling like paper aeroplanes gliding in the sky.

And you have made autumn.

Andrew Thomson (8)
Cawdor Primary School, Nairn

Recipe For Autumn

Take blustery wind taking my hat off,
Frost as cold as ice and as sparkly as glitter.

Add leaves as red as rubies,
Leaves as yellow as sunshine,
Falling like a twisty snake.

And you have made autumn!

Katrina Macarthur (7)
Cawdor Primary School, Nairn

Recipe For Autumn

Take an angry blowing wind blowing through the leaves,
Light, cold, shimmering frost on the grass and trees.

Add a kite flying in the breeze,
Leaves hovering down like little fleas.

And you have made autumn.

Eliza Petrow (8)
Cawdor Primary School, Nairn

Recipe For Autumn

Take big raindrops as clear as glass,
Wind as strong as a wrestler.

Add leaves as red as my coat,
Jumping in leaves like a frog,

And you have made autumn.

Oscar Baird (8)
Cawdor Primary School, Nairn

Locked Up

In my room I have a box,
Full of nasty nightmares.
The box is congested with lurking dragons,
Overflowing with hidden secrets
And jammed with cold-hearted demons.
Those nightmares are full of brutal serpents,
With a passion for blood.
Such serpents with fatal bites
And harsh cries.
Unknown monsters with deafening roars,
Slinking behind rocks,
Ambushing, waiting.
Lethal aliens creep,
Waiting to snap you up,
To pluck you out of infinity.
Poisonous goo oozes out of rocks.
Sinister eyes watch from cracks in mountain sides
And that is why I lock them up,
So they don't threaten my fantasies.
    Sweet dreams!

Ha, ha, ha, ha!

Ailsa Baird   (11)
Cawdor Primary School, Nairn

Recipe For Autumn

Take blustery wind blowing off people's hats,
Glittering frost on the very cold grass.

Add leaves as red as roses,
Falling like a person dancing in Hawaii.

And you have made autumn!

Christina MacIntosh   (8)
Cawdor Primary School, Nairn

I Should Like To . . .

I should like to paint the thrush singing its morning song.
The noise of an owl screeching in the night
And paint the lovely soft breeze as it runs its
Fingers through my hair.

I should like to touch the rainbow
And take a bit home to keep in a jar.
Reach up into the soft fluffy clouds.
Touch the sharpness of a twinkling star.

I should like to take a trip to a distant galaxy
And take photos to remind me.
To take a ride of a shooting star
And to hold a lion that would protect me.

I should like to hear the sun as it shines away
And hear the frost on a winter's morning.
Listen to a book as it tells a wonderful story.

I should like to see what a tiger is thinking
Behind the glow in its eye.
To see the exact moment that a honeybee dies
And see what is going to happen in the future.

Mairi Dutton (10)
Cawdor Primary School, Nairn

Recipe For Autumn

Take blustery swirling leaves blowing in your face,
Cold and grey fog that you can't see through,
Blustery wind blowing scarves in your face.

Add leaves as yellow as the sun shining down,
As gently as my rabbit's fur,
As blustery as a cold and dark night.

And you have made autumn!

Kirsty Stewart (8)
Cawdor Primary School, Nairn

The Forest Of Hidden Lives

A path winds into sun-vented woods that casts eerie
shadows everywhere.
Gnarled old trees seem to stare down on high.
A green slimy pool lies hidden by reeds at the edge of the path.
Pine needles cover the nearby ground in a vast green carpet.

Conkers drop softly onto the dark forest floor.
A bubbling brook burbles over sand and stone segmented
by rushing water.
Broom seeds pop open like popcorn.
Ferns reach up for the light poking through the dark trees.

Red squirrels flit quietly from tree to tree.
Acorns half eaten are left abandoned on the ground.
Distant shooting alerts a nearby pheasant as it erupts into the air.
A small deer flees between the shadows pursued by
its camouflaged hunters.

Dens are hidden by overhanging branches like a mother's
protective arms.
A neglected rope swing dangles from a high bough.
Scuffed ground and footprints show the remains of a cowboy
and Indian battle.
Children's excited voices break the silence as they start
On the expedition for berries.

Rhian Jardine (11)
Cawdor Primary School, Nairn

Recipe For Autumn

Take blustery wind blowing through the trees,
Sparkling frost cold on the grass.

Add leaves as red as roses,
The leaves falling like a parachutist.

And you have made autumn.

Gordon Macarthur (8)
Cawdor Primary School, Nairn

Anger

Anger is black like a very angry,
Camouflaged chameleon eating a black fly.

Sounds like a black widow munching
On her husband.

Tastes as awful as a school dinner
Of chicken curry and semolina.

Smells like a smelly, rotten apple
Being attacked by wasps.

Looks like the ugliest monster in the world.

Feels as if a big monster was sucking your soul out.

And reminds me of the awful war in Lord of the Rings.

Calum Robertson (9)
Cawdor Primary School, Nairn

Recipe For Winter

Take racing rain flying through the air
On dark cold nights.

Soaking wet leaves
On a damp, damp day.

Wind blowing off your hat
On a very windy day.

Add watching a hang-glider
On a freezing cold day.

Someone rushing through the field
On a breezy day.

Richard MacDonald (8)
Cawdor Primary School, Nairn

I Wish . . .

I wish I could jump off the moon and float in space,
Slide a camel's neck and land on salty sore sand,
Fly into space and land on the moon.
I wish I could paint the bright stars in the sky,
The tears of a child's eyes going down her face,
A sky with people parachuting through the clouds.

I wish I could touch the sun as it's setting across the seaside,
The shooting star while it goes zooming past the sky,
Touching thunder without getting killed.

I wish I could feel the earth and see the plants,
The smooth skin of a jellyfish without getting a shock
And feel the heat of the sun.
I wish I could taste the clouds like candyfloss,
A chunk of the moon for cheese.

I wish I could hear the fresh air go past across my face,
The beaming hot sun going right into my ear,
The moon moving past Earth gradually.

I wish . . .
I wish . . .

Adam Hamilton (11)
Cawdor Primary School, Nairn

Anger

Anger is black like a whirlwind going round at
A million miles per hour.
Sounds like an infuriated gorilla going crazy.
Tastes like worms mixed together with dirt.
Smells like a gorilla's armpit with insects under it.
Looks like an alien with eight eyes and ten tentacles.
Feels like a hundred nails going into my body.
And reminds me of the time when I almost drowned.

Craig Smith (9)
Cawdor Primary School, Nairn

Love

Love is pink like a lovely parrot made by my dad.
Tastes like delicious roast chicken.
Smells like strawberry scented shampoo.
Sounds like gentle, delicate music.
Looks like a blueberry muffin just waiting to be eaten.
Feels like sinking my teeth into a big bar of sweet, white chocolate
And reminds me of when my mum gives me a big cuddle.

Eilidh McCulloch (8)
Cawdor Primary School, Nairn

Anger

Anger is red like fire burning down a house.
Sounds like a werewolf howling at the moon.
Tastes like smelly, old socks.
Smells like dirty old clothes that have not been in the wash.
Looks like a skeleton coming upstairs.
Feels like your insides are about to blow up
And reminds me of a stormy night.

Findlay Strain (8)
Cawdor Primary School, Nairn

Anger

Anger is red like a hungry roaring Tyrannosaurus rex,
Sounds like a beating drum in my ear,
Tastes like a rotten brown apple,
Smells like a stinking pig,
Looks like a green alien in a blazing fire,
Feels like a car knocking me over
And it reminds me of when dinosaurs walked the Earth.

Gavin Wilkie (8)
Cawdor Primary School, Nairn

Anger

Anger is red like a bush fire out of control.
Sounds like a newborn baby screaming its head off.
Tastes like hot chilli powder, spicy and hot.
Smells like a person who has just had garlic.
Looks like a dog as it guard its young.
Feels like fire inside my tummy
And reminds me of my mum shouting.

Hannah Jakobsen (8)
Cawdor Primary School, Nairn

Anger

Anger is black like the night sky with no stars.
Sounds like a werewolf howling at the moon.
Smells like drains needing to be cleaned.
Tastes like mustard on a hot dog.
Looks like a lion that hasn't had its dinner.
Feels like a very sore tummy
And reminds me of the hurricane in Florida.

Kalum Turnbull (8)
Cawdor Primary School, Nairn

Anger

Anger is black like a raging gorilla protecting her young.
Sounds like a howling wolf in the night.
Tastes like a tomato and mushy peas mixed together.
Smells like the smelliest disgusting skunk I ever knew.
Looks like two eyes coming towards me in the middle of the night.
Feels like my insides are about to blow up.
Reminds me of when my dog had an accident in my bed, I was angry!

Tilly Hepburn-Wright (9)
Cawdor Primary School, Nairn

Love

Love is as yellow as my granny's sweet canary.
Sounds like a trickle of water in a mountain spring.
Tastes like creamy cheese from France.
Smells as wonderful as the sharp tang of marmalade.
Looks like my noble cat.
Feels like the soft fur of my hamster
And reminds me of my cat Tanera who is sleeping peacefully.

Victoria Laidlaw (8)
Cawdor Primary School, Nairn

Anger

Anger is like two red eyes,
Sounds like a drum in my ear,
Tastes like a spoonful of cod liver oil,
Smells like a rotten banana,
Looks like a red ball of fire,
Feels like someone hitting you inside
And reminds me of leaping flames from a burning bonfire.

Alreis Fairbairn (10)
Cawdor Primary School, Nairn

Anger

Anger is black like a black panther in rage.
Sounds like a howler monkey in a rainforest.
Tastes like a leopard eating a deer.
Smells like a field of dung.
Feels like a hot fireball inside me
And reminds me of my mum yelling at me.

Amie Stewart (9)
Cawdor Primary School, Nairn

Anger

Anger is black like Saddam Hussein's heart.
Sounds like someone dying in great pain.
Tastes like a half eaten rotten plum.
Smells like a pile of droppings with dead flies on top.
Looks like a lion's red eyes.
Feels like your insides are on fire
And it reminds me of when my boiler blew up.

Andrew Fyfe (9)
Cawdor Primary School, Nairn

Anger

Anger is black like a ferocious, stormy night,
Sounds like a snake hissing very loudly,
Tastes like a sour apple,
Smells like a field of dung,
Looks like a crocodile's throat,
Feels like a slithering snake
And reminds me of when my bedroom was a tip.

Ashleigh Macarthur (10)
Cawdor Primary School, Nairn

Anger

Anger is as red as a beetroot,
Sounds like a herd of stampeding elephants,
Tastes like a bar of dark bitter chocolate,
Smells like a jar of smelly pickled onions,
Looks like a raging bull,
Feels like a parrot pecking your head
And reminds me of a herd of charging buffalo.

Brodie Walker (9)
Cawdor Primary School, Nairn

Anger

Anger is red like a wild raging jaguar.
Sounds like a jaguar raging with temper.
Tastes like a smelly dinner from a café.
Smells like a smelly fish.
Looks like a wild, raging rainforest.
Feels like rough rabbit fur
And reminds me of a smelly rotten egg.

Jacquelyn Wilson (9)
Cawdor Primary School, Nairn

Love

Love is like a red, red rose,
Sounds as wonderful as lying on a desert island
With a cup of orange juice,
Tastes like steak in gravy,
Smells as beautiful as strawberries,
Looks as cute as a puppy's frown,
Feels as wonderful as living on the moon
And reminds me of my first skating competition.

Lesley Forbes (9)
Cawdor Primary School, Nairn

Love

Love is red like a magnificent, sweet smelling rose.
Sounds like my favourite pop music.
Tastes like a delicious milk chocolate bar.
Smells like a big, beautiful bunch of lavender.
Looks like my puppy with its cute puppy face.
Feels like lying in a lovely hot bubble bath
And reminds me of when my mum and dad give me a kiss.

Mhairi Docherty (9)
Cawdor Primary School, Nairn

My Dreams

I would like to fly around the world on the back of a unicorn
And visit places I have never been before, like the land of dreams.
To go to the moon on a dragon
And bite a chunk of moonish cheese.

I would like to paint a million aliens at once on Pluto,
The bottom of the ocean
And the tropical fish swimming at the bottom of the ocean.

I would like to taste the colours of the
Rainbow mixed together like hard crystal.
A taste of the clouds like a huge ball of candyfloss.

I would like to take home a gigantic elephant from a safari park,
A dolphin from the North Sea
And place it in my swimming pool for me to see.

I would like to swim like a whale,
Skimming through the spacious oceans of our world
And hop like a frog in a thousand acre field.
To swim in a pool with tropical fish,
Sailing past my eyes.

These would be my dreams.

Lynne Macarthur (9)
Cawdor Primary School, Nairn

Anger

Anger is red like a strawberry about to explode.
Sounds like a big tree crashing down on to the ground with a big bang.
Tastes like a boiling, hot, spicy curry.
Smells like a big skunk.
Looks like a big bull about to charge.
Feels like a long slimy snake wrapping its body around you
And reminds me of a fork screeching on the plate.

Rhiannon Morrison (9)
Cawdor Primary School, Nairn

The Cloakroom

The huge corridor of wet floor stretches into doors
Of tough working children.
It is a road of hooks and coats and shoes.
Open bags like hippos yawning and in all the open bags
There is homework waiting to be done.
The bell goes.
It's all busy again.
Everybody is scrambling to get their piece and play.
It's like a traffic jam of children visiting the toilets
With traffic light people stopping naughty children going in.
There are still some laces being tied.
Chatting children discussing secrets.
Some faces carefree and some sulky faces trying to be cheerful.
The bell goes again.
The children return to the doors of hard work.
Silence.

Simon MacDonald (9)
Cawdor Primary School, Nairn

Love

Love is red like a sweet smelling rose.
Sounds like a bird singing a love song.
Tastes like a piece of Galaxy chocolate.
Smells like my mum's perfume.
Looks like a beautiful garden of flowers.
Feels like lying on lots and lots of flowers
And reminds me of my puppies' cute little faces.

Shanice MacLennan (10)
Cawdor Primary School, Nairn

Lonely Beach

Towering waves
Crash down on the sandy shore.
Impatient gulls wait for the right
Moment to dive at anything offered.
Stranded crabs desperately trying to
Find their way to sea.
A motionless lifeguard just waiting
For something to happen.
The deserted promenade longs for
Someone to stand on it again.
A boat creaks as it rocks
On the disturbing waters.
Abandoned sandcastles sink
Into the slushy ground.

Despised beach
No longer wanted,
No longer played on,
The weather made sure of that,
The wind insists that the tide rules all,
As the tourist season ends
This is my cue to exit.

Michael Ashmole (10)
Cawdor Primary School, Nairn

Anger

Anger is red like an exploding volcano.
Sounds like an angry tiger roaring.
Tastes like a hot dog with mustard and chillies on it.
Smells like sour milk.
Looks like a worm that you had just put on a fishing hook.
Feels like your heart is thumping
And reminds me of very bad weather.

George MacIntosh (10)
Cawdor Primary School, Nairn

Recipe For Autumn

Take a cold evening like the North Pole,
Day as a sparkly frosty disco ball,
Rain is as small as your teardrop.

Add leaves gently flowing in the breeze,
Jumping in the leaves like a kangaroo,
A kite gently blowing in the breeze.

And you have made autumn!

Charlotte MacKintosh
Cawdor Primary School, Nairn

I Would Like To . . .

I should like to ride a dragon around the galaxy.
Go in a time machine and take me into the future.
Take a lump of cheese out of the moon.

I would like to paint the wind talking to the trees.
The sound of a gun shot going off.
The good smell of air freshener.

I would like to take home the sun and the moon.
Take all of my favourite things.
All the puppies in the world.

I would like to be the fittest boy in the world.
Stay up all night.
Be the cleverest in the class.

I would like to do all these things and a lot more.

Billy Aitken (11)
Cawdor Primary School, Nairn

The Peaceful Wood

Gnarled neglected twigs lay at the side of the gritty path.
Gigantic trees tower over the wood like giants guarding the
                                    deep dark woodland.
Honeysuckle covers the air in a heavenly scent.
While,
Red squirrels rustle about in the trees, munching their pine cones.
The long never-ending river whispers to the trees as the fish in and out.
People occasionally catch themselves on the gorse as they
                                    walk down the footpath.
Young deer prance around as their mothers watch them with
                                    careful eyes.
Rabbits run into burrows and flatten the flowers as they hear
Children's voices echo the woods with joyful laughter.
As night falls silence returns once again,
And the rabbits re-emerge.
But the rabbits know that tomorrow there will be more new voices,
Tomorrow . . .

Emma Mackintosh (11)
Cawdor Primary School, Nairn

I Wish . . .

I wish I could slide down one side of the rainbow
And into a pool of psychedelic dreams,
Fly on a shooting star and visit the man on the moon.

I wish I could paint the smell of freshly cut grass,
The sound of birds chirping in the heat of the sun.

I wish I could take home a bag of magic from fairy land,
A piece of cloud that looks like candyfloss,
A jar of planet Mars and eat it on a frosty night.

I wish I could taste a chunk of the moon in a cornet,
A bite of the sun and feel it going into my body.

                I just wish.

Samantha Birkbeck (10)
Cawdor Primary School, Nairn

I Would Like To . . .

I would like to paint the simplest picture without any brush,
The twinkle of a star on a very black sky.

I would like to see the centre of the sun,
The middle of a living tree,
The part of the world where all life began.

I would like to hear the trees' silent voices while in the woods,
The screech of pain from a light bulb when it is turned on.

I would like to take home a chunk of the sun
And a star so bright that the human eye can't look at it,
A piece of the always moving wind in an unbreakable jar.

I would like to ride on top of a shooting star that is going
So fast nobody can see it,
Sit on top of the moon watching all the never dying
Clouds move slowly around the Earth.

Niall McCulloch (9)
Cawdor Primary School, Nairn

Winter

Soft snow plunges down as it carpets the last green land to be seen.
It lays there silky, glistening, as the sun shines.
Robins are flying collecting the ruby-red berries,
Their red breasts attract spectators.
Ice plasters itself in the puddles
And makes the road shine like it has been polished.
People start to skid on the thickly ice-covered ponds.
Birds are whistling and trying to find bread that has been donated.
Sledging tracks are being made,
They look like bumpy slides that are at the shows.
Snowmen are dotted about each garden with their scarf and hats on.
Carol singers going to doors singing festive music
And asking for donations for the poor.
Lights dangle round every house while everyone waits for Christmas,
Great!

Danielle Murray (11)
Cawdor Primary School, Nairn

Sinister Grove

Paths leading to fun and a new adventure
Like a tour round Highlands.
Leaves leave the trees and enter the earth
Like bombs falling from a plane.
Birds advance from a tree to the atmosphere
Like artillery from the army.
Rivers speed into deepness and wood territory
Like rapid rabbits running in a straight line to their burrow.
Pine needles lying on the earth
Like a bed of nails jagging in your feet.
Stones helpless in the liquid
Like wasps to our jam.
Dens being put up for animals' homes
Like houses for human beings.
Winds hit your ear in scary ways
Like a horror film squeezing your fear out.
Trees are overlooking your movement
Like spies planning to take you hostage.
Wildlife prancing and dancing about
Like monsters eating everything in their path.
Grass; nice, rough and long
Like a perfect place for lurkers to hide.
Insects flying and crawling around,
The grove is like a city to them.
The sky blue or red with a sun and clouds
Like a type of fungi mushroom.
Sound of shooting hurts your ears
Like a paper cut in your finger.
Sinister Grove, the entrance to the eerie forest.

Angus Paterson (9)
Cawdor Primary School, Nairn

I Would Like . . .

I would like to catch the rain when it falls to the ground.
To fly a pig round the world.
Bite into the sun and feel it turn to jelly in your mouth.
Swallow the wide and vast ocean.
Sit on a giraffe's head and get the best view
And slide down its sleek neck.
Bounce for the sky and play peekaboo through the clouds.
I'd like to shrink myself and put chalk on my feet,
Step on the blackboard and write everything neat.
I'd like to take a chunk of the moon home for dinner.
I'd take the spooky trees home for our garden.
I'd like to paint the bumblebees buzzing round the plant pots.
I'd like to smell the wind in the trees but I know I can't.

Kate Paterson (11)
Cawdor Primary School, Nairn

Things I Keep In My Heart

I would like to paint the trees in the soft soil.
Draw the scent of the early morning rain as it falls on the lawn.
Paint the taste of the fresh bread on the kitchen table.

I would like to take home the end of the rainbow
And keep the secret to me.
Keep the happiness of a fox hounding a rabbit.
Preserve a chunk of the Earth's crust.

I would like to have a bear that cuddles me every morning
With a bowl full of porridge in her hands.
Admire a monkey that steals all the school books.
Enjoy a laugh with a zebra who charges at the teachers.
And own a giraffe that spies on the neighbours.

Sophie Strain (11)
Cawdor Primary School, Nairn

Winter's Coming

Long narrow paths leading to secret places.
Trees huge and tall,
Like statues.
Flowers blooming up through long grass.
Birds chirping as they fly from tree to tree.
Neglected rope swings sway in the breeze.
Red squirrels scatter up trees.
Pine needles cover the ground like a carpet.
Leaves crunch as you walk.
Conkers fall off trees.
Brambles growing on jaggy bushes.
Grass as green as can be.
Ferns getting knocked over by deer.
Rabbits bouncing around.
Dens that foxes lie in during the day.
Snails lying on mushrooms munching away.
Winter's coming.
Snowdrops fall from the trees like heavy pine cones.
Sticks snapping as you walk along.
Colour of the sky is dark with black but fluffy clouds.
Dogs chase rabbits through thick snow.
Rabbits' burrows are full of frost.
Children play on sledges.
Winter's here,
Winter's here.

Lauren Urquhart (10)
Cawdor Primary School, Nairn

My School Playground

Cheerful children run around
Shouting and laughing with their friends.
While I, sitting on a bench gloomy, abandoned,
No one to play with.
Playground is like a battlefield,
You've got to find your way.
Grass is soaking, sticky,
Shoes are soggy and wet
Running through the enemy line
Looking for someone, pushing, shoving.
People get hurt, kicked, punched,
Elbowed, get into trouble.
What a noise . . . people crying, laughing,
Shouting, screaming.
Got a headache,
Boys and girls playing football,
What a stink coming off them as they run.
Running . . . crash, bang, falling on
The concrete, cut your knee, blood everywhere.
I walk . . . laughing, whispering, sharing,
But sometimes crying, being brave in the face of it all.
I must not stay alone,
I must join a side.
In the battlefield, it's a war,
Sometimes good, sometimes bad,
It depends on who you are
And who you know.

Toni Wilson (11)
Cawdor Primary School, Nairn

My Secret Place

In my secret place
I hide my dreams in a corner.
At night I take them out,
I wish I could ride on clouds
And live up there when I am sad
Or sleep up there in the softest bed in the world.

I wish I could ride on a shooting star
And go to all the planets in the universe.
I wish to have magic powers
Like a witch and turn all the people's worries away.

I wish I could have a dream house
That would keep all my nightmares away.
I wish to have a dolphin
So it can take me to golden dreams.
I wish my golden dreams could come true.

Eilidh Montgomery (10)
Cawdor Primary School, Nairn

1, 2, 3, 4, 5

One wooden woman wore a woolly wig.
Two toy trolls took ten tiny tigers.
Three thin thorns threw thimbles.
Four French footballers found fat friends.
Five funny fish fought fifty frogs.

Gordon Urquhart (7)
Conon Primary School, Dingwall

1, 2, 3, 4

One wobbly wig with wet wellies.
Two tiny tadpoles took tasty toffee.
Three thirsty thieves threw thistles.
Four funny frogs forgot Freddie.

Ethan Bushell (7)
Conon Primary School, Dingwall

1, 2, 3 . . .

One wee witch wanted wellies.
Two tiny tanks taught twins.
Three things thought through thorns.
Four fat footballs fell flat.
Five foolish frogs fixed fences.
Six silly sausages smoking cigars.

Jordan Garden (7)
Conon Primary School, Dingwall

1, 2, 3, 4, 5

One windy winter Wendy Witch was well.
Two tortoises taught teachers to talk.
Three thick thirsty thieves thought.
Four fat fairies found forty foolish fish.
Five friendly footballers fell flat.

Kieran McSwegan
Conon Primary School, Dingwall

1, 2, 3, 4, 5

One wet winter we went walking.
Two tubby twins tried to take two toys.
Three thimbles thought they were thieves.
Four fat frogs forgot football.
Five foxes fired fifty farmers.

Russell Meiklejohn (7)
Conon Primary School, Dingwall

1, 2, 3 . . .

One wiggly worm was in the wood.
Two tiny tubby twins taught tortoises.
Three tasty tigers trundled trolleys.
Four fat fish found footballs.
Five funny frogs fooled French friends.
Six silly sailors stole sixty-six sausages.
Seven smelly socks sitting smoking cigars.

Christopher Urquhart (6)
Conon Primary School, Dingwall

1, 2, 3, 4, 5,

One wolf was watching wiggly worms.
Two tiny trolls told tigers to toddle.
Three thin thorns threaded through thunder.
Four funny fools forgot frogs.
Five frogs found food from foxes.

Michael Gillett (7)
Conon Primary School, Dingwall

1, 2, 3, 4

One wiggly worm went wiggling.
Two tiny twins took ten tigers.
Three thin thieves threw thick thistles.
Four fan footballers found five fairies.

Jack Cuthbertson (7)
Conon Primary School, Dingwall

1, 2, 3 . . .

One windy winter we watched a woolly worm.
Two tiny Teletubbies talked to the table.
Three thin thimbles thread thick things.
Four funny frogs fell from five fat trees.
Five foolish friends found forty fat fairies.
Six slimy sausages sizzling in the sun.
Seven smelly socks stink so Susan sinks.
Eight mats are straight gates.
Nine naughty knickers nibbled ninety nuts.
Ten tubbies take two tortoises to terrible tigers.

Rachel McKay (7)
Conon Primary School, Dingwall

1, 2, 3 . . .

One winter we watched wiggly worms.
Two twins toddled around Teletubbie Land.
Three thimbles thumble thorns.
Four funny fat fishfingers fell for foxes.
Five funny foolish fairies found five French friends.

Rebecca Williams (7)
Conon Primary School, Dingwall

1, 2, 3, 4

One wolf watched a wiggly worm.
Two tiny tots took trouble.
Three thistles threw thorns.
Four fat foxes frightened frogs.

Andrew Forsyth (7)
Conon Primary School, Dingwall

The White Shark

It is so scary
In your mind
Like hundreds of
Teeth straight and fine.

Lots of people get
Killed every year
When they thought
The sea was clear.

But why God made
Them I don't know,
All they're good
For is catching in a show.

No one likes them
Ugly beasts,
But really take care
Or you might be their feast.

Campbell Orr (10)
Corstorphine Primary School, Edinburgh

The Burning Fire

I am a fire burning
In the night, people
Throwing planks of wood,
Rubbish, even some old chairs.

I am a fire burning
In a field, I can see
Some light, I think it is
The farmhouse.

I am a fire burning
Red, yellow, orange and blue,
It is the morning now
And I am just some sparks.

Callum Gibson (10)
Corstorphine Primary School, Edinburgh

My Bed

I love my bed,
I'm glad to go to sleep.
I can't wait to go to bed,
I don't make a peep.

The duvet is pink
With circles of life.
It's like a star in the sky
Up high!

At night I go to bed,
It's where I dream.
Sometimes I wish
That I could get ice cream.

My pillow is pink,
It has lots of colours,
Some are dark
Like you would find in the park.

I love my bed,
There's no doubt about it.
I love my bed lots,
It's like a huge pit of life.

Caitlin Mooney (9)
Corstorphine Primary School, Edinburgh

The Girl Of Sadness

Her face is full of sadness,
I wonder what's wrong,
She is standing in the streets,
Wearing a patched dress.

Oh my word,
She is poor,
I wonder if she needs some help
And needed some warmth in her.

Lucy Belcher (10)
Corstorphine Primary School, Edinburgh

Eistier

Why is he over there, shimmering gently by the stream?
The fading sun illuminates him.
I just see his ghostly figure.
The steam is hissing and sloshing beneath my feet,
Why is he here?

Fully clad in armour,
The phantom warrior lumbers towards something sticking
out of the ground,
He grabs it and takes it from the ground.
I made out the word *Eistier* carved beautifully in the wood
before he faded.

I'm left in the now deserted forest.
I found myself yellow *Eistier,* the light dimmed,
He appeared again,
He grabbed me, I felt I was in the grave.
My blood froze, I fell to the leafy earth,
Dead.

Jamie Snape (10)
Corstorphine Primary School, Edinburgh

Classrooms

I am in the classroom
What can I see?
A pencil like a stick,
A bottle as still as can be
And a board much taller than me!

I am in the classroom
What can I see?
A pencil case like a tin,
A teacher as strict as can be,
Last a computer, just for me!

Anna Wilson (9)
Corstorphine Primary School, Edinburgh

Fireworks

Bang! Whizz! Whoosh!
The fireworks are up in the sky!
Reds, golds, greens and blues
And stars, rockets and wheels.

Ruby red, deep red like blood,
Green as emeralds, shining in the light,
Sapphire blue, blue as the sky,
Golden Catherine wheels, a glitter at night.

It's dark,
The fireworks light up the sky!
Shooting upwards,
Up, up and up.
So far . . . then *bang!*
They explode into a whirl of shimmering stars.

They're great!
Whizz! Bang! Whoosh!
A glimmer and then a sparkle . . .

Then darkness,
They've gone.

Maddie Atkinson (10)
Corstorphine Primary School, Edinburgh

The Man In The Corner

There he was in the corner
His hair dark as the night sky
His eyes as white as a full moon
What was he doing there?
What was he thinking?
He is there all day
He is there all night
I would like to know why.

Rowan Fustukian (10)
Corstorphine Primary School, Edinburgh

In The Dead Of Midnight

In the dead of midnight
I am in a church,
I walk into a room encased with darkness.
Through the cracked window
I see the graves
Almost watching me
Like the burning eyes of fiery demons.
I hear the giant timber door
Creak open and bang! Shut again.
A cold shiver runs down my spine!
My hair stands on end!
With my heart in my throat!
I edge around,
I see a transparent figure.
With a swoop of light
I am the transparent figure haunting the church
In the dead of midnight!

Jamie Duff (9)
Corstorphine Primary School, Edinburgh

Remote Control Planes

How does that little man feel
he's in that plane
it's going to rain
how does that little man feel?

What should I do
what would you?
How does that little man feel?

I'll run away
what about the pay
how does that little man feel?

He's going to smash
crash, crash, crash
I think that little man's dead.

Euan Jenkins (9)
Corstorphine Primary School, Edinburgh

The Happy Lady

I feel very happy
Too good to be true,
I've just won the lottery,
I wish you had too.

I am delighted,
My money, oh gosh!
I'll buy a new house
With all my new dosh.

I'm leaving tomorrow,
What a sad thought,
But I'm very happy
With the house I have bought!

The moving van's here,
I'll pack up and go,
We had a good time
In the winter snow.

The weather was cold,
But now it is dry.
I'll miss my old house,
I'm leaving now, goodbye!

Alistair Buist (9)
Corstorphine Primary School, Edinburgh

The Scottish Flag

You have a blue background
And a white cross.

You fly up high on a big pole,
You're known by the whole of the country.

We all salute you,
You are the flag of the Scots.

You are the Scottish flag.

Ryan McEwan (10)
Corstorphine Primary School, Edinburgh

The Street

I am walking down the street
I wonder what I can see.
I can see a car,
Oh and a school.

I am walking down the street
I wonder what I can see.
I can see a lady get off the bus,
I can see some children play all around.

I am walking down the street
I wonder what I can see.
I can see a teacher,
I can see around.

All the things I have seen
They all are very nice,
I wonder what I'll see tomorrow.

Danielle Brown (10)
Corstorphine Primary School, Edinburgh

The Army Train

The army train running over the hill,
Its back car streaming with smoke,
Running off in the other direction.

Past the wreckage of the tram
And bus, past the truck
I am trapped under,
Through the tunnel,
Right into the enemy's trap
With a *kaboom!*
It was over
And so was the track.

David Booth (10)
Corstorphine Primary School, Edinburgh

They've Gone

I'm alone,
No one's here,
Just me,
Only me.

In the darkness,
In the silence,
I'm standing,
Standing alone.

I listen,
Hear nothing.
I open my eyes,
See nothing.

I'm thinking,
Thoughts run through my head,
All the happiness we had,
All the things they said.

Silence,
Darkness,
They've gone . . .

Ellen Atkinson (10)
Corstorphine Primary School, Edinburgh

My Cats

My cats are soft and cuddly,
My cats are very big,
My cats are heavy,
My cats are brothers,
My cats like attention,
My cats like soft sofas,
My cats catch birds,
My cats catch mice,
I love my cats.

Iain Hall (10)
Corstorphine Primary School, Edinburgh

The Cloud

What is that?
It looks like a bat,
It's high in the sky
And it knows how to fly.

It might be a plane or maybe a bird,
But it's a cloud!
It's a cloud!
It's a cloud!

Then it went *pop!*
I got a big shock.
It just split in two,
I didn't know what to do.

I never know what to do
When things just split in two,
But now the things have gone puffy
And they look sort of fluffy.

Maybe I will spend more time looking at this cloud.

Calum Henderson (10)
Corstorphine Primary School, Edinburgh

The Unlucky Fish

Swim! Swim! Flap your flippers,
He is after me.
Hip, hip hooray I lost him.
What is that shadow?
It floats on the water.
Oh look, a worm, my lunch is free.
Ow a spike,
Help I'm stuck, I'm getting pulled up.
I'm out of the water,
I can't breathe, I can't bre . . .

Sam Ramsey (10)
Corstorphine Primary School, Edinburgh

Seeing Through Others' Eyes

There is a war in my country
When I wake up every day to hear
Screams and bangs.

My sister looks after me
My mum has died, I have no dad
I'm feeling very, very sad.

My younger brother is very ill
I have a chill.
My brother is feeling ill
But we can't afford any pills.

All I see is live or die
That's what goes through my eyes.

I wonder if I am going to live or die
Seeing through others' eyes.

Chanelle Murray (10)
Corstorphine Primary School, Edinburgh

The Battle

I can hear loud footsteps banging like an earthquake
There's people running, shouting, crying
I pull out my sword.

Suddenly the two armies meet, yelling, slashing, killing
My sword falls and it brings me with it
All I can see is blood, guts and armour
The wound in my stomach is bleeding badly.

One army won, we retreated
But I couldn't run
I am almost dead, so bye.

Euan Brockie (10)
Corstorphine Primary School, Edinburgh

The Flying Squirrel

I am meant to be able to fly
But I cannot.
I jump from a branch
And try to glide to another
But I just fall.

I should be able to glide
My mum said
It's just not fair
All my friends can glide
But I just fall.

Then I noticed
I had holes in my flaps of skin
The doctor fixed them
Now I can glide.

Stuart Lindsay (10)
Corstorphine Primary School, Edinburgh

Wavy Tree

The wavy tree
staring at me
you have to wonder
is it scared of thunder
you wouldn't think so
but you never know
the leaves are turning red
the birds are eating bread
I thought it was spring
now the birds are starting to sing.

Ryan Aird (10)
Corstorphine Primary School, Edinburgh

Me

I look up in the sky
And see the clouds so high
They are very bright and white
The same colour as my kite.

I look up in a tree
And see a large blackbird
It is very black
The same colour as my cat.

I really don't know
What's happening to me
The world keeps spinning
Round and round me.

I really don't know if I like my mum
I really don't know if I like my dad
But I know they don't like me
Because I'm not their cup of tea.

They leave me in the house
They leave me in the car
Because they don't like me
I'm not their cup of tea.

Shannon Steedman (9)
Corstorphine Primary School, Edinburgh

Deep Blue Sea

I'm a fish in the sea
I hear the sound of fishing boats
Then I hear this splash
All these bubbles
Then I see this strange thing
In the end my mum tells me
That it was a net
Then Mum told me to
Swim, swim, swim away.

Alasdair Germain (10)
Corstorphine Primary School, Edinburgh

My Life

Worried like a footballer in the World Cup
Scared as a duck coming face to face with a fox.

Being in jail a box for a home
Not getting to call home
Don't have enough for a phone.

I am not getting out
Never getting and about.

Can't go and see
My mum and daddy.

Calum McManus (10)
Corstorphine Primary School, Edinburgh

My Baby Sister

My baby sister is only two months old
She doesn't understand anything yet,
But that's alright,
She's only small.

When people come round,
They gather round her.
They talk to her in a funny way
I sometimes wonder what they say.

Gurgle, google, proogle, froogle
Who's a lovely girl?
Coochy, coochy coo!
Now see what I mean?

But when no one is around
I pick her up,
I kiss her,
She laughs and pulls my hair.

Sometimes she is a bit annoying,
But I really do love her.

Sadaf Sohrabi (10)
Corstorphine Primary School, Edinburgh

The Terrible Dream

I was on my own at the breakfast table
I needed to go to the bathroom
But I did not go.

I wanted to go out somewhere
But the door was locked
And I did not have a key.

I got off the stool and walked into the lounge
When I opened the door I got a terrible fright
When I woke up it was all just a dream.

Avril Rosie (9)
Corstorphine Primary School, Edinburgh

Beautiful

Her eyes were like a bird's
Fishing in a river of dreams
Her skin as soft as a newborn princess.

Her hair was golden and soft
Like the most cuddly chick on the farm
Her voice was as wonderful
As a thousand harps all playing the same tune.

Her dress was as lovely
As a star in the night sky
Her personality was like
A goddess.

I hope that one day I will see her again.

Scott Lindsay (10)
Corstorphine Primary School, Edinburgh

The Woodlouse

I think back to when I was free
Alone in the garden no one else but me

But not anymore
I feel like I've hit the core

People picking me up and putting me down somewhere
The others say they don't care but I care

They have a good look at me from their high spot
Looking at me like I'm a small dot

They moved me from my family and friends
When will it ever end?

Lizzie Welham (10)
Corstorphine Primary School, Edinburgh

My Puppy

My puppy is small
But he is loud
When I go to school
He wants to come too
When I get back from school
He is as excited as a winning performer
And jumps up at me
I am pleased to see him
Like I haven't seen him for a month
I've only had him for a week
That's not very long if you're young.

Katherine Burnet (10)
Corstorphine Primary School, Edinburgh

The Classroom

I'm sitting in the classroom
Wondering what to do
I can tell you one thing
It needs a good broom.

The air is cold and misty
I jump with both feet
I get a fright as the floor creaked.

I want to escape this classroom
There must be something I could do
If there's only magic in the air
I would zap away you too.

Alexandria Rutherford (10)
Corstorphine Primary School, Edinburgh

I'm Thinking

I'm thinking of my mum,
I'm thinking of my dad,

I'm thinking what they're doing,
I'm thinking good and bad.

I'm thinking of the gunshots,
Shooting around my dad,

I'm thinking of my mum
In jail which is bad,

I'm thinking about going back to Dad,
I'm feeling bad, bad, bad!

Shona McDonald (10)
Corstorphine Primary School, Edinburgh

My Violin Story

When I first started playing my violin
It shrieked like a mouse
I tried my very best
But still the squeaking rang through the house.

The next time I went to my teacher
I said I wanted to quit
I'd never make it as a famous musician
Me and a violin just don't fit.

My teacher refused to let me go.
'Play all day and play all night!'
So I did as I was told
And never gave up without a fight.

Right now I feel very nervous
1,000 people are waiting for me to play
I hope I don't play the wrong note
Because I want to come here again some day.

Yvette Rosie (10)
Corstorphine Primary School, Edinburgh

Fish Eyes

I remember when I was swimming
Where it was, joyful in the middle of the sea
With all my friends.

I remember when I was in the fishmonger's
It was so cold and icy
And I just about became a block of ice
Until he came along.

I remember when I was on that dreaded boat
The crew were so nasty on that boat.

I remember when I was eaten up and chewed to the bone
It was dreadful being tossed in the bin
You're lucky you are not me.

Jordan McKay (9)
Corstorphine Primary School, Edinburgh

Why Him And Not Me?

Why does he get all the attention?
No one says anything to me
If I get attention I will feel like
We're getting an extension.

Cousins, aunties, uncles, grannies and grandads
Not one saying hello to me.

'Coochy, coochy coo,' they say to him
Why him and not to me?

Is it because he is small and I'm quite tall?
Is it because I'm thin but he's thinner?
Is it because he's five months old and I'm four years old?
Is it because I've got hair and he hasn't?
Why him and not me?

Scott Edmond (10)
Corstorphine Primary School, Edinburgh

Going To Jail

A while ago people called me a nice man,
No more wrong they could have been,
A while ago I was considerate, caring,
Now no jail lawyers will listen to me,
I'm going to jail and I can't escape it,
So maybe I should just face it.
In jail the food is horrid,
All they ever have is porridge.

Every meal,
Every day,
Every week,
Every month,
Every year,
Everyone.

Robbie Taylor (10)
Corstorphine Primary School, Edinburgh

My Pet Cat

I have a pet cat
He is white
He is called Snowy

He is warm when I hold him
His teeth are like sharp pins

I have a pet cat
I always give him a toy fight

His length is a whole arm
If he could stretch out

He always makes me feel glad
When I am bad

He sleeps on my bed
Or maybe on my head

He sleeps in light
And awakes at night

That's my pet cat.

Selina McPherson (10)
Corstorphine Primary School, Edinburgh

Daydreaming

Staring out the window
Looking at a tree
Hoping that something
Will happen to me
That I will lift off my seat
And fly up higher into the sky
I would wave to my friends
And family
Hoping that they would
Wave back at me
That would be a real treat
If I could fly and lift off my seat.

Caitlin Snell (9)
Corstorphine Primary School, Edinburgh

Is It A Flying Pig

Looking up at the sky
Thinking what it could be!
Maybe it is a giant fly
Or a bee about to sting me!
It is as big as the world
And shiny like mum's new car!

Looking up at the sky
Thinking what it could be!
Maybe it is a blackbird
Staring straight down at me!
It is as long as a train
And as high as the white, fluffy clouds!

Looking up at the sky
Thinking what it could be!
Maybe it is a flying pig
But it really can't be!
It is so big and so long
I don't know what it could be!

Claire Paxton (10)
Corstorphine Primary School, Edinburgh

The Night Bird

Night-time in the dark, dark woods
Down in the valley
Watching a bird flapping its wings
Staring down at me.

I am thinking about it
But is it thinking about me?

Does it think about its mum
Or is it thinking about its dad
I do not know, but I am glad
I'd better get home to my mum and dad.

David Provan (10)
Corstorphine Primary School, Edinburgh

Lost Girl

I'm lost
Up the valley
Through the glen
I'm scared
I wonder when I can clear off home again
Frightening sounds all around me
I wonder when they will find me
It's very dark, stars in the night
Might I be helpless for the rest of my life?
I haven't got might
I haven't got muscle
To find food should I hustle and bustle?
I don't know what to do or how long to wait for you
My shoe is torn
My dress is mucky
My hair is very yucky
I'm not very lucky.

Hannah McCall (10)
Corstorphine Primary School, Edinburgh

I Hope

I am a shark
I live in the Pacific Ocean
I would like to go deep down in the ocean
I would like to go hunting with Dad

I want to meet a blue whale or a dolphin
I want to know what that fish is doing
I wish I was as big as the ocean
I hope those fishermen don't catch me

I hope!
I hope!

Steven Leahey (10)
Corstorphine Primary School, Edinburgh

Fish Bones

I am lying in a bucket
And I dream back to when I was alive
When I was swimming in the sea
When I was captured by a big net
And taken onto a big ship.

There I was hit in the head
And put into a big, cold freezer
Oh yes I dream, dream, dream
Then there was the time when I was . . .

Taken and suddenly chopped to bits
With a big, big knife
Then put onto a plate and given to a man
Who ate me.
Now I just lie in the bottom of a bin
And dream, dream on.

Stephanie McKenzie (9)
Corstorphine Primary School, Edinburgh

Small

How come I'm so small
And everyone is so big and tall
I wish I could be as tall as them
Instead of being as small as the tip of a pen.

With my small, tubby legs
And their tall, skinny legs
They are so out of this world
And mine are so down in this world.

They have a funny stick in their hands
And they put it down to paper
What is this strange thing
Maybe I'll find out later!

Hannah Marshall (9)
Corstorphine Primary School, Edinburgh

I'm A Baby

I'm a baby, I'm a baby,
What a wonderful thing.
My mummy and my daddy,
Just bring, bring, bring.
But the problem is,
I just can't talk.
The problem is,
I just can't walk.

I'm a baby, I'm a baby,
What a wonderful thing.
My mummy and my daddy,
Just bring, bring, bring.
I play with my toys,
I play with my teddies,
I play with my froggies,
That are called the Freddies.

I'm a baby, I'm a baby,
What a wonderful thing.
My mummy and my daddy,
Just bring, bring, bring.
I feel so happy,
So I stand up and walk.
I feel so excited,
So I start to talk.

I'm a baby, I'm a baby,
What a wonderful thing.

Ellie Blair (9)
Corstorphine Primary School, Edinburgh

Sad Little Girl

Eyes like an angel's,
But as sad as an injured dog's,
No fancy tops for her,
No high heeled clogs.

A sad, lonely child,
Alone in the world,
People walk past her,
Their lips curled.

Poor little girl,
Sad little girl.

She does not go to school,
Where's her mum and dad?
She does not have a home,
She is very sad.

She sleeps in a run-down car,
With a sleeping bag and toy,
She saw a small person,
It was a little boy.

Poor little girl,
Sad little girl.

The boy had his dad,
His dad had him.
The little girl's still sad,
She misses her mum and dad.

Poor little girl.

Natasha Wyllie (10)
Corstorphine Primary School, Edinburgh

My Night Of Fright

It was a strange night
Looking here, getting a fright
Looking there on that cold, cold night
What was that strange noise?
Oh, maybe it's just some boys
I'm just being silly
Oh no!
I'm lost!
'I can help you,' said a voice,
'I can take you home in my Rolls Royce.'
Off I go
Way off back home.
I'm glad I'm back
And back on track.

Reem Ryanne (9)
Corstorphine Primary School, Edinburgh

My Great Bed

My bed is as comfy as a leather sofa
My bed is as soft as a fluffy white rabbit
That just had a bath.

My bed is my favourite thing
And I sleep in it most of the time.
At night I go to sleep in it
I feel like a queen.

When it is time to go to bed
I feel happy that I can go to sleep
And get energy.
As strong as a very, very jumpy kangaroo.

Beth Mooney (9)
Corstorphine Primary School, Edinburgh

Make Up Your Mind

Recycle! Recycle!
Save the world.
Recycle! Recycle!
Save the trees.
Recycle! Recycle!
Please, please, please.

Recycle! Recycle!
Save the bears.
Recycle! Recycle!
Where is the love?
It came from above
So please recycle!

Recycle! Recycle!
Keep our Earth clean.
Recycle! Recycle!
Don't be mean to the snakes,
As they swim in the lakes,
So please recycle!

Isabell Lee (10)
Craigbank Primary School, Larkhall

Where Is The World?

Where are the trees?
Where are the blue seas?
Where are the whales we used to see?

Recycle your paper we want to live
Put your bottle in the blue bin.
Do you see we're saving the world?

Recycle your cans
For more aluminium
So we can make more cars.

Graham Rock (10)
Craigbank Primary School, Larkhall

Everywhere

See the fish in the water,
Some are thin and some are fatter.
Throw a stone into the water
See the fish they all scatter.

See the birds in the air
Go and help them, don't be square
Every day in the air
See the birds take a share.

See the bears on the land
Lions, tigers, make a stand.
Caterpillars, worms and hares
Why just stand there?
Give a hand!

All the animals mentioned here
They're endangered. Help them stay.
Stop the shooting everyone,
Help the animals every day.

Robbie Wells (10)
Craigbank Primary School, Larkhall

The Birds

Stop, listen, the birds are singing
Stop, listen, hear the birds.
Stop, listen, hear the nice birds.
Stop, listen, look at the sky.

Some birds like to fly
Some birds don't.
Some birds like to coo
And some birds don't.

Shereen McEwan (10)
Craigbank Primary School, Larkhall

Beneath The Lake

Beneath the lake was an old, crinkled up letter
and this is what it read;

'Beneath the lake, beneath the lake,
if you swam in it, it would be a big mistake.
Although you don't know he is awake,
creeping slowly under the boat,
there he is, keeping afloat,
he's so shiny he's just like tin
but the smell of him is like a bin.'

The boy has a smile on his face while fishing,
the next he screams and is gulped under the lake.
Splash!
The lake goes silent and from that day on
the lesson was learnt, never to go *beneath the lake!*

William Marshall Miller (11)
Craigbank Primary School, Larkhall

Life On Land

Don't go hunting, never shoot
for the ones that are cute.
Stop hunting, start caring
stop killing, stop tearing.

Leopards lie and hunt their prey
foxes and cubs run around and play.
Birds in the air flying high
it's a shame to see them die.

Baby seals crying for their mums
are being killed in their tonnes.
So for all God's creatures everywhere
be aware of that trap and snare.

Craig Williams (10)
Craigbank Primary School, Larkhall

We're On The Trees' Side

Trees, trees, I love them
Trees, trees, I love them
Trees, trees, are they important?

Trees, trees, they are fun
Trees, trees, they are fun
Trees, trees, where's the sun?

Trees, trees, don't kill them
Trees, trees, don't kill them
Trees, trees, why bother killing?

Trees, trees, we need you
Trees, trees, we need you
Trees, trees, give us paper.

David Marshall (10)
Craigbank Primary School, Larkhall

Polluted Seas

The pollution in the sea
affects the animals that we see
like fish and birds, whales and turtles
sharks and dolphins, newts and seals.

Stop causing the pollution.
Please! Oh please! Oh please!
You're killing the animals in the sea
that we like to see.

Every animal in the sea
deserves to live, can't you see?
It's us who's killing them.
Please stop it, just please.

Marc McGinty (9)
Craigbank Primary School, Larkhall

Save The Earth And Animals

Watch the sea,
What can you see?
I see animals sick
From the oil in the sea.
What can we do?

Look! Look!
What can you see?
I see oil in the sea.
What will happen to the animals?
What can we do?

Don't leave rubbish,
Recycle everything you use,
Don't put rubbish in the sea.
Save the animals, that's what we can do,
What can we do?

Charles Brady (9)
Craigbank Primary School, Larkhall

Don't Throw Away!

Wait! Stop!
Don't throw away.
It will be useful
for another day.

Wait! Stop!
Don't throw away.
Put it in the bottle bank
for another day.

Wait! Stop!
Don't throw away.
Recycle everything you've got
for another.

David Lyden (9)
Craigbank Primary School, Larkhall

Where Is The Love?

Animals are our friends
Pollution is our foe
If it doesn't end
Where will we go?

Big boys in the street
Picking up a gun
Think that it is neat
To kill birds for fun.

Leave the snakes' skin
Never hit or batter
They need their skin
You think it doesn't matter.

Where is the love
For the animals I see?
Who will take care of them
If not you and me.

Damien McQueen (10)
Craigbank Primary School, Larkhall

We Love Trees

Why do people chop down trees?
They only go to waste!
Trees! Trees! Trees!

Why do people chop down trees?
They've not harmed you or me!
Trees! Trees! Trees!

Trees work hard,
They don't sit around,
Trees! Trees! Trees!

Andrew Mayberry (9)
Craigbank Primary School, Larkhall

Recycle

Come on, it's time to recycle,
Everyone on their bicycle,
Drop the rubbish in the bin,
You can even put in tin.

Plastic, paper that will do,
Everyone will say, 'Phew.'
There is a bin everywhere,
Don't just stop and stare.

So now you know, recycle junk,
Don't just lie in your bunk.
Go to the bin every day
And shove your rubbish all away.

Christopher Cole (9)
Craigbank Primary School, Larkhall

We Are On The Trees' Side

Stop using trees
We need oxygen.
I like birds singing to me
Up a wonderful tree.

Look! Look at that wonderful tree.
It's so nice and fresh
That's how it is to me.
You are fresh to me.

Look! Look at the trees
Like me
On the trees
So it's fresh.

Kane Bennett (9)
Craigbank Primary School, Larkhall

Conserving The Planet

Remember! Remember!
Don't throw rubbish on the ground,
use the recycling bin.
Remember! Remember!
Don't kill the animals
would you like it?

Remember! Remember!
Don't cut down trees,
we need them for fresh air.

Jordan Hollands (9)
Craigbank Primary School, Larkhall

Can You Guess Who I Am Yet?

I'm lurching in the bushes
And creeping around at night,
Always eating and never sleeping,
Can you guess who I am yet?

I prance and pounce,
Weighing more than an ounce,
Always looking for prey,
Can you guess who I am yet?

I have spots and dots
And loads of knots,
Always coughing up fur balls,
Can you guess who I am yet?

My fur is so long,
It's like a sarong,
Covering all of my body,
Can you guess who I am yet?

I wait till it's time,
To go and dine
And then I catch my prey,
I bet you can guess who I am now!

Karen Taylor (11)
Falla Hill Primary School, Fauldhouse

Another Busy Day

The sun has risen, it's morning now
And the monkeys are ready to play.
The animals have woken from their slumber,
Ready for a brand new day.

After about an hour or so,
The rainforest is full of life,
The jaguars are hunting, watching for prey,
Baring their teeth as sharp as knives.

Snakes slither on the ground,
Macaws fly up high.
Colours fill the whole rainforest,
From the ground to the sky.

The sloth climbs the giant trees,
Taking his own pace.
The lion sits bolt upright,
Protecting his family and place.

The hummingbird collects the pollen,
From all the beautiful plants.
All the trees are covered,
With millions and millions of ants.

It's dark now and the animals are tired,
And really need their beds.
So they settle down for another night
And rest their weary heads.

Laura Dodds (11)
Falla Hill Primary School, Fauldhouse

Rainforest Life

The trees of green and the long grass full,
The monkeys hop and swing from here to there,
The grass is full of insects and spiders,
But the river is always still.

The lions pounce on their prey for food,
The babies roll and play at the riverside,
The snakes slither and hiss through the fallen leaves,
Birds and butterflies flutter and swoop from tree to tree.

The canopy covers the whole forest,
It is full of colour and leaves,
But the river is always still.

Leigh Salmond (11)
Falla Hill Primary School, Fauldhouse

The Rainforest

T oucans fly fast through the air
H ummingbirds hover to catch their prey
E lectric eels swim in the water and electrify anything that's in

R are plants sniff and smell of the morning rainforest
A nimals are making noises in the trees
I nsects run about the grass and sometimes fly
N aughty monkeys swing in the trees making noises
F ancy plants look so beautiful and colourful
O rang-utans are a little fat with a six pack on their chest
R ainforests are full of trees and always full of animals and plants too
E lephants are big and shoot water out of their spout
S nakes slither across the grass
T igers duck and hunt for their prey.

Jordan Kelly (11)
Falla Hill Primary School, Fauldhouse

Nature's Song

Through the leaves of the tallest trees,
A blaze of sunshine wisps through the breeze.
The symphony of a bird's call soothes my ears,
With the snake's hiss and the monkey's cheers.
The rain sounds a rhythm on the moist ground,
I'm mesmerised by the sound.
The hummingbird is singing its song,
Not a single note is wrong.
The leaves shake in the wind and whisper a secret,
Never known by you or I.
Now the forest falls silent, the song is over,
Finished with the toucan's cry.

Stephanie Roden (11)
Falla Hill Primary School, Fauldhouse

The Rainforest

T he rainforest is so bright and colourful,
H issing snakes cover the ground,
E lephants roar and fill the place with water.

R are birds screech and chirp all day,
A nts scurry across the floor hunting for their food,
I nsects run and hide all over the place,
N oisy monkeys fill the trees.
F lowers fill the area with colour and brightness,
O rang-utan swing from tree to tree,
R eptiles pounce and walk all around,
E lectric eels swim and slither in the river,
S loths hang and climb up the trees,
T igers roar and chase the other mammals.
                    The rainforest is a beautiful place.

Abby McKay (11)
Falla Hill Primary School, Fauldhouse

The Rainforest

Rainforest, rainforest, why are you so tall
And evergreen from summer to fall?

Rainforest, rainforest, you hold so much rain,
In your hot and hostile terrain.

Rainforest, rainforest, acres of beautiful trees,
Lions and hummingbirds, ants and bees.

Rainforest, rainforest, butterflies take flight
And lions bite when given a fright.

Rainforest, rainforest, you are full of rain,
But what you do not feel is sadness and pain.

Rainforest, rainforest, the bugs and the bees,
The beautiful skies, the beautiful trees.

Rainforest, rainforest, why are you not cold?
You are so mighty, beautiful and bold.

Derek Smith (11)
Falla Hill Primary School, Fauldhouse

Rainforest

Rainforest, rainforest, look how green you are!
Rainforest, rainforest, how many trees do you have?
Rain, rain in you, but it is nice for you, to make you grow.
Rainforest, rainforest, how many fruits do you have in a year?
Rainforest, rainforest, what kind of animals do live with you?
I know! I know! What kind of animals live in you -
Snakes, lions, tigers, monkeys, elephants, ants, leopards
And gorillas.

Jordan McDonald (11)
Falla Hill Primary School, Fauldhouse

The Rainforest

R ain, rain always rain splashing on the trees' leaves
A lways hot and humid down on the ground
I nsects running all over the place
N oisy birds squawking away, you'll never know what to say
F ar and near all over the place
　　　　　you might even say you're lost in space
O n the trees swing the monkeys and chimpanzees
R oaring tigers, buzzing bees, there's lots of sounds from the trees
E lephants, swimming in the water they like to make a splash
S nakes and salamanders all around you'll need to watch your step
T oucans squawking all around as if it's the tiger's prey.

Emma Merrilees (11)
Falla Hill Primary School, Fauldhouse

The Rainforest

Rainforest, rainforest, covered with leaves,
Home for the animals who live in your trees.

Rainforest, rainforest, how beautiful are you,
Bright and colourful and full of life too.

Rainforest, rainforest, full of noise,
Rainforest, rainforest, full of choice.

Rainforest, rainforest, what can I say?
Rainforest, rainforest, just as the day . . .
Ends.

Laura Swan (11)
Falla Hill Primary School, Fauldhouse

The Amazing Rainforest

R ainforests are covered in trees,
A nts crawl across the ground,
I nsects run all over and hide,
N oisy animals cover the trees,
F lowers cover the rainforest in colour,
O rang-utans swing from tree to tree,
R eptiles pounce about the rainforest,
E lephants roar and blow water about,
S loths dangle from the trees,
T igers pounce really far.

Colene Copland (11)
Falla Hill Primary School, Fauldhouse

Where Are You?

Animals live in the place so proudly,
Monkeys call from the trees so loudly,
Huge spiders scuttle across your feet,
To get to the other side to see who they meet.
Insects as big as dinner plates buzz around your ears,
While crying massive tears,
They have no fear cos they've lived there for years.
Enjoying it all the time,
Never committing a crime.
Where are you?
In the rainforest?
Yes!

Ellie Lamont (10)
Falla Hill Primary School, Fauldhouse

Rainforest

R ainforest, rainforest, covered with trees,
A nts crawling across the ground,
I nsects crawling everywhere,
N oisy birds flying about,
F rogs jumping in the air,
O rang-utans hiding in their homes,
R ain is hitting off the trees,
E lephants stamping their feet,
S loths swimming in the water,
T igers climbing up the trees.

Ashley Smillie (10)
Falla Hill Primary School, Fauldhouse

The Beach

Seagulls circling the beach,
Swooping towards food.
Waves crashing against rocks,
Footsteps in the sand.
Salty water in my mouth,
Ice cream dripping down my hand.
Seaweed smelling in the sun,
Feeling the water cold, but nice.
I think the beach is a great place to be!

Cara Targett-Ness (7)
Flora Stevenson Primary School, Edinburgh

The Beach

The wind making ripples on the water,
People trying to catch jellyfish,
Swimming fish popping up,
Seaweed floating on the waves,
Happy children playing.

Aaron Heinemeier (7)
Flora Stevenson Primary School, Edinburgh

The Beach

Smooth shells all different colours
Washed up by the sea.
Hear the sound of squawking seagulls
And the happy sound of shouting people.
The bitter taste of the salty sea
But the lovely taste of ice cream just for me.
Smell the seaweed and the lovely fresh air,
Feel the touch of soft sand
Covering my hands and all over me.
I really like the beach,
It's the best place ever.

Anna Hale (8)
Flora Stevenson Primary School, Edinburgh

The Beach

Big waves covering small rocks,
Seagulls screaming and swooping,
Cool water tickling my tongue,
Smells of the slimy seaweed in the water.
I love the beach in summertime.

Duncan Player (8)
Flora Stevenson Primary School, Edinburgh

The Beach

Calm waves slapping against the rough rocks,
Cold ice cream dripping down my hand,
Little fish dancing in the water,
Twinkly sand in-between my toes.
I love the beach in the summertime.

Nadia Unis (8)
Flora Stevenson Primary School, Edinburgh

My World And Me

My world and me
Is so much to me.
My mother and father
Grandparents and aunties.
I have got a whole life ahead
Until I'll be rightfully dead.
So I won't kill myself with poisonous lead.

My world and me,
So special to me.
You come if you care
Or don't even dare!
No one notices that it's beautiful,
With lilies, roses and daffodils.
It's full of education, life and conversation
And a whole big blast of co-operation.

The only people there,
Are the ones who really care.
If you want to disrupt my world
Don't you even dare!
You can fly around the twisted clouds
And breathe the freshest air.
I allow any famous people, just like Tony Blair.

Ye Ye Xu (9)
Flora Stevenson Primary School, Edinburgh

The Swimming Pool

Children splashing,
The whistle blowing,
Floats bobbing,
Lifeguard watching,
Red eyes stinging,
The pool is the best place to be.

Mark Jarvis (7)
Flora Stevenson Primary School, Edinburgh

Ten Things Found In A Mermaid's Hair

A tangled jellyfish,
An old dirty shell,
A letter from a sailor,
A singing crab,
A little piece of lime rock,
A baby merman,
A very scaly fish,
A hidden eye,
A map that none could understand,
A pen that nobody could work.

Ella Duffy (7)
Flora Stevenson Primary School, Edinburgh

Sea Mammals

Leap of dolphin,
Song of whale,
Gliding porpoise,
And dugongs sail.
Sea mammals can be found
In water, beaches and all around.
Underwater unicorns are narwhals,
Harp seals cannot make music
But beautiful white fur.
Sea mammals can be found
In water, beaches and all around.
But they are hunted for
Meat, skins, body parts and more.
Sea mammals are trying to help man.
Let us help them as much as we can.

Varshini Vijayakumur (7)
Flora Stevenson Primary School, Edinburgh

Water

Floating, boating on the sea,
It goes splosh,
I use it to wash,
It's water,
It's water.

In the sink or in the sea,
It's still water you will see.
The waves go splash,
The boat goes swish
And all around are fish.

Rebecca Morton (8)
Flora Stevenson Primary School, Edinburgh

Ten Things Found In An Old Shed

A web with flies on it and a spider creeping around.
A broken toy box from when I was young.
Old shovels used by my great-grandpa.
A rake to sweep leaves.
Baby toys from when I was small.
An old china vase covered in spiders.
A smashed glass.
Dried-out flowers from Mum's last birthday.
An old radio that my sister had.
A one-eyed teddy bear.

Jenny Docherty (8)
Flora Stevenson Primary School, Edinburgh

Sport

S port is fun and it keeps you fit
P eople can do their own little bit
O n the pitch or in the pool
R ugby and swimming are really cool
T ennis is my number one and it is truly lots of fun.

Hannah Watson (10)
Flora Stevenson Primary School, Edinburgh

The Day Sandy Got Out Of His Cage

The day Sandy got out of his cage,
Mum was in an awful rage.
She blamed it on the little kid,
Who really nothing at all she did.
Poor Zoe started to cry,
I bet she wished that she could fly
Happily out of the room
All the way to the big moon!
We had two hamsters, one called Sandy,
The other ones fun name was Andy!
Someone opened Sandy's door,
And that (of the hamster) was the last we saw.
A photo of him is in the frame,
The little one, on it his name.
When Sandy made his great escape,
A mystery person in a cape
Went into the room and opened the door
But then the person did no more
Except one thing I'll say to you,
He crept right to him and said, 'Boo!'
He gave poor Sandy such a fright
He ran into the dark, cold night.
Wonder how I know all this stuff?
See the person who did it was me!

Caitlin Lewis (9)
Flora Stevenson Primary School, Edinburgh

How Could Children Be So Rude?

How could children be so rude?
Slurp their drinks and gobble their food,
Throw their soup at their mums,
Chuck chocolate at their dads,
And beyond measure, suck their thumbs
Chew some paper, eat some mud,
Drop some paint upon their mother's son,
        say their sister is a thug,
Try to murder their pet dog!
How could they be so rude?

Lily Roberts Thomson (9)
Flora Stevenson Primary School, Edinburgh

Space

Space has loads of planets
and lots of twinkling stars.

These planets are all different,
and the red one is called Mars.

Space has loads of secrets
that we just do not know

But since it is so far away
not many people go.

Space has loads of stars
that are very, very bright

But all these stars stay hidden
until day turns into night.

Aidan Targett-Ness (9)
Flora Stevenson Primary School, Edinburgh

Haunted Hallowe'en House

Come in if you dare,
You might get scared
By vampires, ghosts and skeletons.

Come in if you dare,
You might be a frog in a second,
By the witch called Speller.

Come in if you dare,
A ghost might go in you
And a vampire might suck your blood.

You might die of fright
So I advise you do not come in, but . . .
Come in if you dare!

Paul Oglesby (10)
Flora Stevenson Primary School, Edinburgh

The Rainforest

A swish of leaves,
The hiss of a snake,
The crack of a nut,
The hum of a hummingbird,
The splash of fish,
A gorilla beating and bashing its chest.
The roar of a jaguar,
The squawking of a toucan,
A spider scuttling across the rainforest floor,
And that is all the noise you hear today.

Lauren Anderson (9)
Flora Stevenson Primary School, Edinburgh

The Rainforest

Listen to the sounds I hear,
The hiss of an anaconda,
The splash of a fish,
A monkey screaming, *ooh, ooh, ooh!*
Hot, humid air swishing all around,
The darkness reach out to hug you,
Dangerous lions roaring
Hummingbirds singing,
Lots of trees swishing,
The wind roaring and howling,
The rain falling, *pitter-patter, pitter-patter,*
Dirty puddles splashing,
Pigs grunting,
Cows running and running away,
The madman laughing.

Nicole Calder (10)
Flora Stevenson Primary School, Edinburgh

The Rainforest

I listened to the horrid howler monkey wailing like a baby,
The trees swooshing, swaying in the breeze,
The rain dribbling, dripping off umbrella leaves.
I listened to the flap-flapping flying falcons,
The dense, dark, dangerous forest,
The hot, humid, heavy air.
I listened to the buzz-buzzing bouncy bees,
The river splishing-splashing on its way to the sea,
The leaves flap-flapping in the wind,
The sun shining and making me blind.
I listened to the jumping jaguar, which is hard to race,
The rainforest is a *lovely place!*

Katie Brown (9)
Flora Stevenson Primary School, Edinburgh

My Mummy

My mummy's eyes are like the summer sky.
Her hair is like sand on a beach.
Her lips are like red, red roses.
Her nose is like an icy ski slope.
My mummy's teeth are like stars in the sky.

Chiara Crawford (8)
Flora Stevenson Primary School, Edinburgh

I Know Someone Who Can . . .

I know someone who can . . .
Swim faster than a blue whale,
Build quicker than Bob the Builder,
Defeat a cheetah at cards,
Travel the world at the speed of light.

I know someone who can . . .
Beat Albert Einstein in a maths competition,
Cross the Sahara Desert,
Swim up and down the river Nile,
Climb up and down the Grand Canyon.

I know someone who can . . .
Fix things in a blink of an eye,
Demolish Mike Tyson in a boxing championship,
Win a race faster than you say 'Wow,'
Can write 50,000 words in one minute.

I know someone who can . . .
Beat Tiger Woods in golf,
Jump over the Pacific Ocean,
Save a boat from sinking,
And that someone is me.

Michael Venters (10)
Granton Primary School, Edinburgh

I Know Someone

I know someone who can . . .
Climb Arthur's Seat in three seconds,
Do 600 sit-ups and want to do more,
Eat a plate of spaghetti Bolognese and
Spit it back out just like it was before.

I know someone who can . . .
Beat a dinosaur in a fight
Store more food in their cheeks
Than a hamster
Have more legs than an octopus.

I know someone who can . . .
See through your skin
Count to one thousand
Fly without wings
And that someone is me!

Alexzandra Morrison (11)
Granton Primary School, Edinburgh

The Dark

The dark is a name
written in black.

The dark is a dove
leaping through the sky.

The dark is only a feeling
scared and nasty too.

The dark is a God
casting its spell.

The dark is only fantasy
filled with ghosts and ghouls.

The dark is the world
and that's the way it is . . .

Billy Robertson (9)
Granton Primary School, Edinburgh

I Know Someone

I know someone who can . . .
Jump over clouds
Do a wheelie for a year
Swim for 15 miles
Do three forwards flips off a wall.

I know someone who can . . .
Eat dog biscuits
Draw faster than God
Do a whole maths book in 15 minutes
Roar louder than 15 lions.

I know someone who can . . .
Kick a football over the highest building
Run faster than a Ferrari
Shout louder than everyone
And that someone is me!

Michael Hutton (10)
Granton Primary School, Edinburgh

Once Upon A Rhyme

In the morning I say my prayers,
Then I have a game of dares,
When at school, I wait at the gate
For my buddy to be late.
In the class I have mental maths
With my teacher Mrs Paths.
At playtime I climb the hill
To be hidden from Rachel Pill.
After that I do some reading
And some leading for my weeding.
When at lunch I wait in a queue for the loo,
After lunch I have PE with my teacher Mrs D
When at home, I eat my dinner with a sinner.

Ashleigh Gorman (8)
Holy Family RC Primary School, Winchburgh

Once Upon A Time

Speed is multicoloured like a bright rainbow,
Speed sounds like a horse bucking,
Speed tastes like the Monaco Grand Prix,
Speed smells like fuel from a car,
Speed looks like a blurry sight,
Speed feels like wind going past you,
Speed reminds me of myself,
I like speed!

Garry Paterson (9)
Holy Family RC Primary School, Winchburgh

Once Upon A Time

Laughter is green like the long smooth grass,
Laughter sounds like children giggling in the playground,
Laughter tastes like a bowl of ice cream,
Laughter looks like a big round bubble,
Laughter smells like a box of soap powder,
Laughter feels like the friendship between countries,
Laughter reminds me of a clown riding a tiny bike,
I love laughter.

Rebecca Telfer (8)
Holy Family RC Primary School, Winchburgh

Once Upon A Rhyme

Darkness is black like the night sky,
Darkness sounds like a grey theatre,
Darkness tastes like an avocado,
Darkness smells like black smoke,
Darkness looks like luscious dark chocolate,
Darkness feels like grey leather,
Darkness reminds me of my school chair.
I don't like darkness!

Ben Gallagher (8)
Holy Family RC Primary School, Winchburgh

Once Upon A Rhyme

Happiness is pink like a love heart,
Happiness sounds like children laughing,
Happiness tastes like strawberries,
Happiness smells like a cake with pink icing,
Happiness looks like stars in the black sky,
Happiness feels like a newborn baby puppy,
Happiness reminds me of my cuddly mummy,
I think happiness is wonderful.

Laura Simpson (9)
Holy Family RC Primary School, Winchburgh

Once Upon A Rhyme

Love is pink like a rose
Love sounds like a soft piano
Love tastes like creamy caramel
Love smells like a big flower
Love looks like two people kissing
Love feels like a big hug
Love reminds me of my mum
I love love!

Iona O'Hanlon
Holy Family RC Primary School, Winchburgh

Once Upon A Rhyme

Anger is red like the Devil from Hell,
Anger sounds like a car screeching to a halt,
Anger tastes like vindaloo curry,
Anger smells like rotten manure,
Anger looks like an enraged bull,
Anger feels like wasted energy,
Anger reminds me of when my football
Team looses a match,
I hate anger!

Sean Finnigan (8)
Holy Family RC Primary School, Winchburgh

Once Upon A Rhyme

Happiness is silver like a star up in the sky
Happiness sounds like horses trotting on the gala day
Happiness tastes like Smarties ice cream
Happiness smells like plain chocolate
Happiness looks like a face smiling
Happiness feels like picking flowers for Mum
Happiness reminds me of my mum taking
                              me to the park
Happiness is fun for a day.

Caitlan Philbin (7)
Holy Family RC Primary School, Winchburgh

Speed

Speed is red like fire,
Speed sounds like a motorbike,
Speed tastes like sweets,
Speed smells like gas,
Speed looks like the world is moving,
Speed feels like I'm getting blown away,
Speed reminds me of fast water,
I love speed!

Ciaran Reddington (7)
Holy Family RC Primary School, Winchburgh

Darkness

Darkness is black like a long train tunnel,
Darkness sounds like ghosts coming upstairs,
Darkness tastes like green kiwi fruits,
Darkness smells like Bonfire Night,
Darkness looks like midnight,
Darkness feels like cold ice,
Darkness reminds me of Hallowe'en night.
I hate darkness.

Shauna Green (6)
Holy Family RC Primary School, Winchburgh

Excitement

Excitement is yellow like the sunflower,
Excitement sounds like children laughing,
Excitement tastes like strawberry ice cream,
Excitement smells like chocolate candy,
Excitement looks like Smarties,
Excitement feels like my birthday party,
Excitement reminds me of children playing together,
I like excitement.

Megan Dalton (6)
Holy Family RC Primary School, Winchburgh

Speed

Speed is gold like copper,
Speed sounds like a noisy motorbike,
Speed tastes like scoffing a chocolate,
Speed smells like gas,
Speed looks like a flash,
Speed feels like air rushing past me,
Speed reminds me of sports day.
I love speed!

Matthew Stirling (6)
Holy Family RC Primary School, Winchburgh

Happiness

Happiness is red like a giant balloon,
Happiness sounds like children laughing,
Happiness tastes like green broccoli,
Happiness smells like Cadbury's chocolate,
Happiness looks like the teacher when I finish my work,
Happiness feels like doing something special with my mum,
Happiness reminds me of swimming in Spain,
I like happiness.

Jessica Rooney (7)
Holy Family RC Primary School, Winchburgh

Laughter

Laughter is green like the long, smooth grass,
Laughter sounds like children giggling in the playground,
Laughter tastes like a bowl of ice cream,
Laughter looks like a big, round bubble,
Laughter smells like a box of soap powder,
Laughter feels like the friendship between countries,
Laughter reminds me of a clown riding a tiny bike.
I love laughter.

Ryan Green (10)
Holy Family RC Primary School, Winchburgh

Happiness

Happiness is yellow like a busy bee on its journey for honey,
Happiness sounds like children laughing and playing,
Happiness tastes like a sweet ice cream,
Happiness looks like a massive smile,
Happiness smells like home-made jam, cooking,
Happiness feels like a silk dressing gown,
Happiness reminds me of my family and friends,
I like happiness!

Sarah Howard (10)
Holy Family RC Primary School, Winchburgh

Calm

Calm is a transparent colour like a river,
Calm is the gentle sound of a raindrop hitting a puddle,
Calm tastes of cool, cold tap water,
Calm looks like an easy flowing burn,
Calm smells like the seaside,
Calm feels like slipping into a hot bath,
Calm reminds me of the Mediterranean.

Connor Sinnet (10)
Holy Family RC Primary School, Winchburgh

Happiness

Happiness is yellow like a bright yellow butterfly,
Happiness sounds like a flying aeroplane,
Happiness tastes like spaghetti Bolognaise,
Happiness looks like a tiger jumping up and down,
Happiness smells like a sunflower,
Happiness feels like an omelette cooking in a frying pan,
Happiness reminds me of playing with my friends.
I love happiness!

Declan Rennie (11)
Holy Family RC Primary School, Winchburgh

Sadness

Sadness is like the sky on a dull day
Sadness sounds like someone dying
Sadness tastes like the most horrible medicine on the planet,
Sadness looks like a house burning down,
Sadness smells like pepper sauce,
Sadness feels like you have lost your best friend,
Sadness reminds me of a bird that has just died.

Ryan Buchanan (10)
Holy Family RC Primary School, Winchburgh

Speed

Speed is silver like a fish in the sea,
Speed tastes like Turkish Delight,
Speeds sounds like a bell ringing through the day,
Speed looks like a sports car shining in the sunlight,
Speed smells like the tarmac of a racing track,
Speed feels like a hot car door,
Speed reminds me of me.

Connor Gallagher (11)
Holy Family RC Primary School, Winchburgh

Love

Love is red like a robin's chest,
Love sounds like the water rippling,
Love tastes like sweet melted chocolate,
Love looks like two red roses next to each other,
Love feels like a fluffy pillow,
Love reminds me of birds flying in the sky.
I love love.

Yasmin Buchanan (10)
Holy Family RC Primary School, Winchburgh

Happiness

Happiness is yellow like the hot summer sun
Happiness sounds like excited children in the playground
Happiness tastes like sweet candyfloss
Happiness looks like a child's smiling face
Happiness smells like a scented flower
Happiness feels like a waterbed
Happiness reminds me of a giant ice cream cone
I like happiness.

Ruairidh Gauld (11)
Holy Family RC Primary School, Winchburgh

Anger

Anger is dark red like lava pouring out of a volcano,
Anger sounds like a boiler overheating,
Anger tastes like hot ash,
Anger looks like a swarm of locusts eating away at crops,
Anger smells like manure freshly spread over fields,
Anger feels like the burn of an iron,
Anger reminds me of a bull full of rage.
I hate anger.

Jamie Griffiths (9)
Holy Family RC Primary School, Winchburgh

Excitement

Excitement is blue like the sky on a hot day,
Excitement sounds like happy children playing and laughing,
Excitement tastes like an ice cream sundae on a hot day,
Excitement looks like a carnival with lots of shows and balloons,
Excitement smells like a trip to the seaside,
Excitement feels like sitting on a beach on a hot day,
Excitement reminds me of a circus with lots of funny things,
I like excitement.

Blair O'Hanlon (10)
Holy Family RC Primary School, Winchburgh

Silence

Silence is white like the snow
Silence sounds like a blank tape
Silence tastes like a small sweetie
Silence smells like a tiny fragrant flower
Silence feels like walking on thin air
Silence reminds me of a baby mouse
Silence is so quiet!

Caitlin Rose Coyle (10)
Holy Family RC Primary School, Winchburgh

Laughter

Laughter is red like a balloon
Laughter sounds like a crow crowing
Laughter tastes like popping popcorn
Laughter looks like someone going to burst
Laughter smells like fish and chips
Laughter feels like being tickled
I love laughter!

Calum Telfer (9)
Holy Family RC Primary School, Winchburgh

Noise

Noise is grey like the stormy clouds,
Noise sounds like people screaming at the same time,
Noise tastes like bitter sweets,
Noise looks like people screaming every time,
Noise smells like fire,
Noise feels like being shouted straight in the ears,
Noise reminds me of the world wars because
Of the bombing and gun's firing,
Noise is irritating!

Jillian Angelique C Marin (10)
Holy Family RC Primary School, Winchburgh

Love

Love is red like the planet Venus
Love sounds like birds chirping on a cloudless summer's day
Love tastes like sweet candyfloss
Love looks like a small bouquet of flowers
Love smells like sweet lavender
Love feels like butter melting in your heart
Love reminds me of two robins on a winter's night
I love love.

Marina McLean (10)
Holy Family RC Primary School, Winchburgh

Darkness

Darkness is black like the inside of a volcano without any lava
Darkness tastes like creamy dark chocolate
Darkness smells like a musty room
Darkness looks like a gloomy graveyard
Darkness feels like thick black clouds
Darkness reminds me of a new blackboard
I hate darkness!

Natalia Donnelly-Kay (9)
Holy Family RC Primary School, Winchburgh

The Fat Cat

There once was a very fat cat,
Who went to sleep on a mat,
He started to snore,
Got hit by a door,
Then put on a very big hat.

Adam Mullen (9)
Knightsridge Primary School, Livingston

The Very Fat Rat

There once was a very fat rat,
Who thought he was a cat,
He licked his fur,
And liked to purr,
And on the mat he ate a rat.

Connor Salmond (9)
Knightsridge Primary School, Livingston

The Snail In The Pail

There once was a very fast snail
Who fell in a very large pail,
He thought he was dead,
Had a throbbing sore head,
In the pail was a pint of ale.

Shannon Hagan (10)
Knightsridge Primary School, Livingston

Cool Cat

There once was a very cool cat,
That had a very weird hat,
He went to the stage,
And lost his wage,
And fell on a bouncy mat.

Andrew Wishart (9)
Knightsridge Primary School, Livingston

Fluffy Sheep

There once was a fluffy sheep,
Who made an extraordinary leap,
He fell over a stile,
And ran a mile
And fell into a river so deep.

Ryan Egan (10)
Knightsridge Primary School, Livingston

The Absurd Bird

Once I saw a big nest
Covered in a very big vest
Along came a bird
Who thought it absurd
But decided to take a rest.

Alexander Rowland (8)
Knightsridge Primary School, Livingston

The Fork And The Spoon

There was once a lady from Spain,
Who turned into an aeroplane,
She fell from New York
And turned into a fork,
So she never did that again.

There was once a man from the moon,
Who turned into a wooden spoon,
He fell from the sky,
Into an apple pie,
And flew away in a hot air balloon.

Jordan Troup (10)
Knightsridge Primary School, Livingston

Cats And Dogs

There once was a very weird cat,
He was very greedy and fat,
He ate more than his fill,
He came very ill,
And that was the end of that.

There once was a very big dog,
He liked to run and play,
He was running so fast,
He always came last,
Because he fell over a log.

Jordan Laing (10)
Knightsridge Primary School, Livingston

The Cat In The Hat!

There once was a very fat cat,
Who tried to wear a hat,
The hat didn't fit,
So he went for a sit,
Because his head was very fat.

Darryl Beveridge (9)
Knightsridge Primary School, Livingston

The Silly Whale

There once was an enormous whale,
Who went for a very big sail,
He chased some crill
And hit a grill
And almost cut off his tail.

His son was a silly young whale,
And tried to cut off his tail,
He caused a flood,
Which was full of blood,
And started an extremely long wail.

Shawn Oliver Wright (9)
Knightsridge Primary School, Livingston

A Whale In Ginger Ale

There once was a very small whale,
So small he could fit in a pail,
He tried to swim,
But broke his fin,
He was swimming in ginger ale.

Dale Kennedy (8)
Knightsridge Primary School, Livingston

Excitement

Excitement is yellow like the sun
Excitement sounds like the sea swishing in the sun
Excitement tastes like Irn-Bru bubbles on my tongue
Excitement smells like Struan's deodorant.

Andrew Komar (9)
Lamington Primary School, Biggar

Sad

Sadness is the colour of the deep blue sea,
Sadness is the sound of the heavy rain battering off the ground,
Sadness smells like a rose with the sun blazing on top,
Sadness looks like the sun shining onto the muddy water,
Sadness feels like the sand going,
Through the gaps in your fingers,
Sadness remind me of the silver in your eyes.

Craig Gibson (9)
Lamington Primary School, Biggar

Paranoid

Paranoid is red like the blazing sunset in the sky,
Paranoid sounds like black coal crackling in the fire,
Paranoid tastes like a sour berry in my mouth,
Paranoid smells like pepper in my dinner,
Paranoid looks like cheese melted on toast,
Paranoid feels like soft clay going hard in my hands,
Paranoid reminds me of my mum being stressed from the housework.

Stephen McKnight (11)
Lamington Primary School, Biggar

Relaxed

Relaxed is a nice bright yellow of the sun,
Relaxed sounds like Norah Jones on your CD player,
Relaxed tastes like a nice long drink of freshly squeezed lemonade,
Relaxed smells like ice cream that has just come out of the freezer,
Relaxed looks like someone sunbathing on a beach in Spain,
Relaxed feels like your body cuddled into an oversized cushion,
Relaxed reminds me of having a dip in a nice cool pool.

Ruth Bowman (9)
Lamington Primary School, Biggar

Paranoid

Paranoid is like a few flames in a fire,
Paranoid sounds like an earthquake crashing through the city,
It tastes like sour grapes that are two months old,
It smells like sour poisonous berries,
It looks like a purple mouldy banana on your sandwich,
It feels like flames licking your body,
It reminds me of an angry fire in the grate.

Richard Crosby (9)
Lamington Primary School, Biggar

Happiness

Happiness is yellow like a ripe banana sitting in a bowl,
Happiness sounds like the leaves on the trees swishing in the wind,
Happiness tastes like a sweet kiwi ripening for you and me,
Happiness smells like the fresh air blowing outside,
Happiness looks like people playing and having fun,
Happiness feels like a soft cuddly toy that's smiling at you,
Happiness reminds me of a nice summer's day
When everyone is smiling.

Emma Craig (11)
Lamington Primary School, Biggar

Happiness

Happiness is bright yellow, the colour of the sun
Happiness sounds like happy children playing in the sun,
Happiness tastes like fresh strawberries and cream,
Happiness smells like the newly grown grass in my garden,
Happiness looks like the newborn lambs playing in the field,
Happiness feels like a warm summer's day.

Daisy Fox (9)
Lamington Primary School, Biggar

Calm

Calm is blue like a peaceful sea,
Calm is like small waves lapping onto the golden sand,
Calm is like a freezing ice cream on a hot summer's day,
Calm is like fresh water out of a flowing stream,
Calm is like a clear sky on a warm day,
Calm is like a fluffy new blue blanket,
Calm reminds me of a dove tweeting and flying in the clear sky.

Claire Pilpel (11)
Lamington Primary School, Biggar

Sad

Sad is pale blue like the sky in the morning,
Sad is like a blueberry muffin in the freezer,
Sad smells like the cold air in the winter,
Sad looks like the only snowdrop in the spring,
Sad feels like cold water in the Rockies with the snowcapped peaks,
Sad reminds me of someone dying.

Lewis Loening (11)
Lamington Primary School, Biggar

Anger

Anger is red like a fierce exploding volcano,
Anger is like a boiling pot,
Bubbling on the stove,
Anger is like hot chillies
From India,
Melting your mouth
Fierce and red.

Anger is like a
Lightning storm,
Anger smells like burning,
Smoking hot rubber.
Anger is like hot ashes,
Smouldering quietly.
Anger reminds me of my mum
When she is in a bad mood!

Struan Collin (11)
Lamington Primary School, Biggar

Cheerful

Cheerful is like the shining sun
That glows in the sky
It sounds like birds tweeting as
They fly in the air
Cheerful smells like bright red
Roses that shine in the sun.

It looks like a horse running in the wild,
Cheerful feels soft like a cuddly toy
From The Bear Factory,
Cheerful reminds me of my mum,
And dad when they tuck me in at night.

Elizabeth McLatchie (11)
Lamington Primary School, Biggar

Loneliness

Loneliness is like a blue parrot lying limp and forgotten on the floor,
Loneliness sounds like space, no sound at all, just emptiness,
Loneliness tastes like a sour lemon, not welcome to your heart,
Loneliness looks like a badly treated dog,
Shivering in a corner dreading its owner's return,
Loneliness feels like turning for help
But every time having a door shut in your face,
Loneliness reminds me of dead trees,
Slowly rotting away into nothing.

Kieran French (11)
Lamington Primary School, Biggar

Disappointed

Disappointed is like the dark blue colour that sits
At the bottom of the sea.

Disappointed sounds like the slamming of a door.

Disappointed tastes like the hot jalapenos that get
Put in your nachos.

Disappointed smells like the hot smoking bonfire
That burnt all the coal.

Disappointed looks like the hot boiling lava that
Makes you cross.

Disappointed feels like a carrot that's been snapped in half.

Disappointed reminds me of the volcano that
Exploded on Hallowe'en night.

Ellie McGill (11)
Lamington Primary School, Biggar

Upset

Upset looks like the pale blue sky,
Upset tastes like a pale blue fish,
Upset smells like a dead ox tongue,
Upset feels like a soggy wet glove,
Upset sounds like the whistling wind.

Cameron Murdoch (8)
Lamington Primary School, Biggar

Betrayal

Betrayal is black like a black widow spider
Killing its prey,
It sounds like thunder banging in the meadow,
It tastes like peppermint toothpaste burning your tongue,
It smells like black smoke blowing over the country,
It looks like a fire burning rubber,
It feels like a strong burning inside,
It reminds me of my dog's burning black fur.

Tara Jackson (10)
Lamington Primary School, Biggar

Relaxation

Relaxation is purple like a flower newly bloomed,
Its sound purring happily in the sun,
Relaxation smells like a new flower blowing
Gently in the breeze,
Relaxation looks like someone dreaming in a hammock,
Relaxation feels like a fresh new bed cover.

Callum Cross
Lamington Primary School, Biggar

My Magic Box

(Based on 'Magic Box' by Kit Wright)

I will put in my box . . .
The wish of a swimming pool,
I will put in my box . . .
My violin and play in the sun
I will put in the box . . .
A horse, a beautiful horse
I will go riding and jumping at night.

I will put in my box . . .
The wish of a kitten
In a little basket
Which I can play with and
It would roll over.

Rachel Green (9)
Maryculter Primary School, Aberdeen

Spiders

One dark and stormy night,
I don't know what creeps up behind me,
Then one night I saw it!
I ran straight up to my bed,
I hid under the covers for a while,
It crawled under the covers,
I got my mum to squish it,
I thought I was safe so I clambered out,
I saw tonnes of hairy, creepy, black, eight legged spiders,
I hid in the toilet,
Forgetting that that's how spiders get in,
One climbed on my leg. Argh!
Then I fainted with fright.

Robyn Martin (10)
Maryculter Primary School, Aberdeen

Insects

I *hate* insects
Spiders . . . wasps . . . bees
Even daddy-long-legs,
When I was six I used to think
They had eight eyes and were really hairy too.
I wonder why they're always black?
My dad always says, 'They don't touch you,'
But I think they do.
I *hate* all insects except ladybirds and butterflies,
I've *liked* ladybirds since I was five.

I like the colour red and black together
And butterflies are really nicely coloured,
Pink, purple, red, blue - any colour.

Emma Anderson (11)
Maryculter Primary School, Aberdeen

Anger

There's dark green all around me,
There's thunder in the sky,
I am angry all over, I want to swat a fly,
I feel like a kitten just about to die!

Now there's light green all around me,
There are grey clouds in the sky,
I am irritated I just want to sulk,
I feel like stomping my foot.

Now I am seeing yellow, it smells really good,
I see a hopeful future buzzing in my head,
Now I am feeling superb,
I am off to have some food.

Philip Green (10)
Maryculter Primary School, Aberdeen

Cars

Cars revving down the road
At such a flying speed
Watch out for them when you're crossing the street,
Or else you may be dead,
So when you're walking down the pavement,
Watch out, they'll have your head,
You really must listen to what your parents said.

Jamie Graham Pryde (9)
Maryculter Primary School, Aberdeen

FC Barcelona

When I entered the stadium, it felt so empty and cold
And around the stadium I could see a sea of blue seats
As soon as everyone came, the atmosphere was electric
And in the biggest stadium in Europe,
I could hardly bear the noise,
When Barcelona scored it was like standing behind a jet engine,
And at the end we could hardly get out,
What a day!

Calum Reddish (11)
Maryculter Primary School, Aberdeen

The Cool Box
(Based on 'Magic Box' by Kit Wright)

I will put in the box . . .
The moment my baby brother is born,
A pirate on a broomstick,
My Xbox on a boat,
A cowboy in a truck,
A goblin on a horse,
A witch on a dragon.

Cameron Porter (7)
Maryculter Primary School, Aberdeen

The Enchanted World

Step through the mirror glass
Into the world of enchantment,
Unicorns grazing in the fields,
Witches and wizards flying in the
Sky on their broomsticks.

Step through the mirror glass
Into the world of enchantment,
Dragons and trolls blowing fire and stamping.

Step through the mirror glass
Into the world of enchantment,
On the ground little elves and pixies,
The grass made out of gold and silver.

I would always go there again.

Abby Martin (8)
Maryculter Primary School, Aberdeen

Posey

My pet Posey, she ain't much of a rosy,
And she's a big fluffy lump too,
But sometimes she goes crazy
And when she'd done with you
Your vision will be hazy,
And you won't be out of bed for a week,
She is very lazy and she lives in a hut,
She is a thief among the animals,
Stealing all their food
Have you guessed what a posey is?
Posey is a sh . . . ?

Matthew Davidson (11)
Maryculter Primary School, Aberdeen

It's A Dog's Life

I am as swift as a cyclist, flying down the hill
I chase after rabbits, as fast as I can,
They are treats which I often relish,
I run through the fields where the sheep try quite hard to avoid me.

I bark in the night at the birds which swoop through the skies,
Once in the night, I chased a little black cat up a tree,
But the most exciting piece of my history is when I
Ran up the road and killed the neighbour's chickens.

So, that is the prospect of country life from a dog,
My name is Zeb, I'm a Jack Russell terrier,
Yes, maybe to your surprise, but all of those stories were true.

Scott Gammie (10)
Maryculter Primary School, Aberdeen

My Personalities

I don't like to travel,
I don't know why,
It must be my marbles,
I don't know why,
I like to watch TV,
This time I know why,
That's why I have square eyes.

I like Lego,
That's why I like to build,
I like to build,
That's why I fiddle,
I have a bicycle,
That's why I cycle,
This is what makes me who I am.

Callum Boxall (9)
Maryculter Primary School, Aberdeen

Dark Doom

(Based on 'Magic Box' by Kit Wright)

I will put in the box . . .
A piece of gold of the shining star,
The biggest piece of silver of the shining light.

I will put in the box . . .
A guitar of gold shining every day and night.

I will put in the box . . .
A gold dragon sitting on silver.

I will put in the box . . .
A mug made out of bronze.

I will put in the box . . .
Some football goalposts made out of gold.

Connor Flewker-Barker (9)
Maryculter Primary School, Aberdeen

My Magic Box

(Based on 'Magic Box' by Kit Wright)

I will put in the box . . .
A piece of silver of the shining star,
A beautiful horse that can sing.

I will put in the box . . .
A cowboy catching a bull of light,
A piano of gold.

I will put in my box . . .
A wizard that will catch the darkness,
A piece of gold of a comet.

Diderik Van Loon (9)
Maryculter Primary School, Aberdeen

About My Best Friend

She has big eyes,
That always shine
I like them a lot
They are very nice
I can't stop looking at them
She has big ears that I like
She always has a smile
So she always laughs.

Carmen Gammie (7)
Maryculter Primary School, Aberdeen

My Teacher

My teacher is very nice
Her hair hangs down her shoulders
My teacher has beautiful eyes
If I have worries I will tell her
My teacher wears nice skirts
She wears a big smile too
But when we go on school trips
She always needs the loo.

Kirsten Pryde (7)
Maryculter Primary School, Aberdeen

Untitled

My special thing is my dog
It's called Sammy
I play with him all day
He is 13 years old
We feed him all day
We give him water
We care for him
My brother plays outside
When I am giving him food and drinks.

Isabel Van Loon (7)
Maryculter Primary School, Aberdeen

My Magic Box

My mum had a magic box,
She never seemed to use,
So on her 30th birthday,
She sneaked it in my room.
So when I found it in my drawer,
Oh my gosh, what shall I do?
So when we were on our way to Inverness,
I shouted 'Yahoo!'
I put my piano in it,
So that I could play,
I put my big purple ring in,
That slipped off every day,
So I had to put it in my box,
So I wouldn't ever lose it,
So when I got to Inverness,
By my piano I did sit.

Sarah-Ann Stewart (7)
Maryculter Primary School, Aberdeen

My Box

(Based on 'Magic Box' by Kit Wright)

I will put in my box . . .
My soft smooth black cat
My two grey dogs
My four big horses
I will shut the lid.
The next day I will wake up and open the lid,
Put a witch on a black horse,
Candyfloss and play,
On all the rollercoasters at a fair,
A big ride, then go home with all my favourite things.

Kirby Brown (7)
Maryculter Primary School, Aberdeen

My Best Friend

My best friend is kind
And very, very friendly
She has hair like me
Except it is brown
She is only seven
Eight in October
My best friend is good
At swimming, disco and highland dancing
I am good at it too.

Fiona Sutherland (8)
Maryculter Primary School, Aberdeen

Cheetah

They creep
They jump
From tree to tree
They can give you a fright
They are very spotty
They run through grass
I love cheetahs.

Sophie Glass (7)
Muirtown Primary School, Inverness

Sadness

Sadness is red
It smells like fire
It feels
Like you're
Dying
It tastes like blood.

Ryan Junor (8)
Muirtown Primary School, Inverness

Jellyfish

I sting you straight
Watch out for me
Keep away from me
Let me swim straight
I live in the sea
Watch out for me
I'm going to scare you
I must warn you
I'm dangerous
You wouldn't like to see me
I'll make you shiver and shake
You will not like me at all!

Chloe Clark (8)
Muirtown Primary School, Inverness

Getting Ready

I get out of bed,
I get my clothes on,
I go downstairs,
I have my breakfast,
I go back upstairs,
I do my face, teeth and hands,
I get my school bag,
I go to school,
I see no kids,
It's Saturday!

Dionne Macpherson (8)
Muirtown Primary School, Inverness

Owls

Owl, owl hooting in the tree,
Sitting in the tree branch,
Just singing to the beat,
Listening to the fireworks in the park,
Sitting on the tree,
Flying from tree to tree,
Hunting for mice, rats and rabbits,
Flying very high nearly over the moon,
Listening very clearly and soon finding dinner,
Whoosh! Whoosh!
Flying back to his tree.

Rhianna Sturrock (8)
Muirtown Primary School, Inverness

The Ref

Gets changed
Goes to the tunnel
Onto the pitch
Whistle ready
No players!

Reece Paterson (8)
Muirtown Primary School, Inverness

Girls

G ood
I ncredible
R ight all the time
L ovely
S pectacular.

Emma MacRae (8)
Muirtown Primary School, Inverness

Anger

When I am angry, my face goes red,
Anger tastes like some red sauce,
It smells like a bunch of hay,
It looks like a rabbit,
It sounds like a spider,
It feels like a box in my mouth.

Megan Mackay (8)
Muirtown Primary School, Inverness

The Shops

The shops are good
Oh! It has lots of food
Wool and other stuff
Never mess up the shop.

Gillian Graham (7)
Muirtown Primary School, Inverness

Summer

Vest top
Shorts on
Sandles on
No sun!

Leah Goodwin (8)
Muirtown Primary School, Inverness

Grumpy

The colour is black
It tastes like burnt chips
It smells like smoke
It looks like an old fire
It feels like I've broken my arm.

Richard Mackenzie   (7)
Muirtown Primary School, Inverness

Children

C razy
H yper
I ntelligent
L oud
D angerous
R emember
E njoying
N asty plus naughty plus nice.

Ian Findlay (8)
Muirtown Primary School, Inverness

Jelly

Jelly is
So nice
I love it
Quivering, shivering
Wibbly, wobbly.

Steven Milligan (8)
Muirtown Primary School, Inverness

Fear

Colour of fear is black and red,
Fear tastes like sour milk and
Smells like bleeding cuts,
It looks like someone crying,
Because their pet died and sounds like thunder,
It feels like a snake.

Jemma Hogan (9)
Muirtown Primary School, Inverness

Mouse

It scutters along the kitchen floor,
It got chased by a cat round and round,
Tries to get cheese by tip-toeing across the floor,
In the night going into their holes, faster and faster,
Being caught by a cat, it tries to get out but not!

Gavin Hanigan (8)
Muirtown Primary School, Inverness

Sad

The colour is gold and pinky
And it smells like cheese and it
Tastes like a fresh apple on a tree.
It looks like a ball getting run over and
It sounds sad.

Mark Donaldson (8)
Muirtown Primary School, Inverness

Cats

Cats hunt,
Cats play,
Even when
They run away.
Cats have kittens,
Cats blast cause
They're very fast,
Whilst they're hunting
For food to have.
Miaow - purr!

Erin MacDonald (8)
Muirtown Primary School, Inverness

Dogs

Dogs chase cats
Dogs jump on the bed
Dogs scratch
Dogs bite and bark and bark and bark.

Liam Martin (7)
Muirtown Primary School, Inverness

Angry

Angry is red
It tastes like hot and spicy
Chicken with sour curry
It smells like a barbecue on fire
It looks like a devil poking someone
Angry sounds like a woman
Screaming for help
Angry feels like fire burning
Through your skin
Angry is not happy.

Jordan Mitchell (8)
Muirtown Primary School, Inverness

Grumpy

The colour of grumpy
Is black and grey
It tastes like juices
It smells like burnt chips
It looks like a shoe
With custard on it
The sound of my
Mum yawning in the morning
It is horrible.

Steven Keenan (8)
Muirtown Primary School, Inverness

Dancing

Stage out
Kilts ready
Music on -
Teacher here
No dancers!

Rhona Stark (8)
Muirtown Primary School, Inverness

Happiness

Happiness is purple
I am so happy I want to scream the house down
It tastes like blackberries
I am over the moon
I am very happy
It smells like oranges
With the birds flying in the sky
It sounds like a rabbit jumping
It feels like an apple.

Eilidh Beaton (7)
Muirtown Primary School, Inverness

Roses

I
Love roses
Because
They are
Nice
They smell
Like sunshine.

Kaiya Slaney (8)
Muirtown Primary School, Inverness

Sadness

Sadness is red
It tastes like
Walking the
Street with
Your head down
It
Smells
Like
Kicking
On
Your
Head
It
Feels
Like
Lonely
It
Sounds like
Sadness.

Kieran McCann (7)
Muirtown Primary School, Inverness

Dead Worms

Worms are slimy
They live in mud
Birds always eat them
And they eat mud too
Most people fear them
And some people don't
They are so slimy
Some people scream.

Neal Cameron (8)
Muirtown Primary School, Inverness

My Dad And The Cat

My dad
Is fat he
Likes
The cat
The cat is fat too
The cat
Scratched
My dad
My dad
Scratched
The cat
They had

A	fight
It	was
Quite	bad
Dad	hurt
The	cat
The	cat
Hurt	Dad.

Jack Sutherland (8)
Muirtown Primary School, Inverness

Blue Stuff

Baby is coming
Buy blue clothes
Buy blue diapers
Buy blue pram
It's a girl!

Ewan Gault (8)
Muirtown Primary School, Inverness

All's Not Lost

Because I'm blind, because I'm deaf
Does not mean that I'm not able.

I'll shout it to the heavens,
I'll shout it to the world -
Just because I'm blind and deaf
Does not mean that I don't have feelings.

I can sing, I can read,
But I cannot see
Nor can I hear.
But I don't care,
I am *happy!*

All's not lost because I'm blind, because I'm deaf,
I'm well!
I'm happy!

Calum Laing (10)
Prestonfield Primary School, Edinburgh

I Am Deaf

I was not born deaf,
Just because I am deaf now
Doesn't mean
I can't understand you.

It's only some people
Who'll talk to me now.
I do feel upset about it
But there's nothing I can do.

It's not just me who is deaf
There are lots of deaf people in this world.
I can do lots of the things
That you can do.

Adele Evans (10)
Prestonfield Primary School, Edinburgh

Being Disabled

Why do some people laugh at me,
Stare and make fun of me?
Just because I'm in a wheelchair
Doesn't mean I'm any different.

Why do some people ignore me?
I see my friends and say, 'Hi,'
But they just walk away.

It isn't fair that I'm left out
From other people's games,
It isn't fair that I'm ignored
And no one pays attention
To what I have to say.

Yes, I am different.
Yes, I am proud
And, of course, I am able.

Luke Bovill (10)
Prestonfield Primary School, Edinburgh

I Can't Walk

I can't walk,
People look at me.
They don't ask me how I feel,
They ask the person pushing me.

What is wrong with these people?
Why not ask me?
Is there something wrong with my speech?
They should ask me.

Am I invisible?
I don't think people see me.
Is there something wrong?
I'm me,
I am me!

Louise Reilly (10)
Prestonfield Primary School, Edinburgh

I'm Dumb But That Doesn't Mean I'm Stupid

People ask me questions,
I answer back in sign language.
They ask again, a bit louder,
I do the same back.
This carries on until
They're screaming at me,
But still I do the same.
Eventually they're walking off
Muttering to themselves,
'That person's dumb'
Meaning that I'm stupid.

I wish that I could talk,
Let people know how I feel,
Answer questions people ask.
At school I find it hard -
The teacher asks a question,
I know the answer
But I just can't tell it.

Most people find out about my problem
But just look at my disability,
Not who I am,
Which is why I don't have friends
To help me.
It's not me with the problem.
I can do other things too.
It's 'normal' people who have the problem -
They steal, destroy, murder and ruin our environment.
Disabled people don't do things like that,
We care about our world.

Lisa Caldwell (10)
Prestonfield Primary School, Edinburgh

Disabled

I am disabled,
Dis*abled*.

I can't speak

But I can run, I can jump,
I can see, I can hear,
I can read, I can write,
I can feel.

I can be happy, I can be sad,
I can be angry, I can be tired.

I can be tired of people saying,
'Don't bother to talk to her,
She can't answer.'

I can be tired of people thinking,
*I'm better than her because
She can't speak and I can.'*

I can be tired of people ignoring me,
Pretending I'm not there.

I can be tired of people acting like I'm stupid
As if, just because I can't speak,
I can't think.

I can't speak
But I can do so many other things.

I can't speak
Not with my mouth
But I can speak with my hands.
Can you do that?

Why do people concentrate
On what you can't do?

I am disabled,
Dis*abled*.

Christina Connolly (10)
Prestonfield Primary School, Edinburgh

Don't Call Me Stupid

Just because I can't see the world
Doesn't mean I'm stupid.
I can still do everything I did
Before it happened.

I'll bet you can't read
In Braille.
What you can do
I can do too,
But I know I'm different
'Cause I can't see.

I'm embarrassed
By the way some people think of me,
But they should be ashamed,
Not me.

I'll live my life
Proud to be *me,*
and that's the way
It's gonna be!

Thomas McGinty (10)
Prestonfield Primary School, Edinburgh

My Future Is Blind

I hate my disability
Because when people look at me
That's all they see.

I can sing,
I can write,
I can talk,
I can read, I can listen,
I can feel.

You've probably noticed
I'm blind,
I hate it.
Most people ignore me
As if I'm not there.
I hate it when my friends say,
'Did you see that great goal?'
They know I'm blind.

I wish
I could have
My sight back.

Craig Cockburn (10)
Prestonfield Primary School, Edinburgh

Disabled Or Not, It Makes No Difference

I am disabled,
I cannot walk.
I may have a wheelchair
But I am just the same,
Just the same as everyone else.

People may say I look weird.
I am *not* weird,
I am just a normal person,
A normal, kind person.

People treat me differently,
Differently to everybody else.
I am not different,
I'm *me!*

I wish I was accepted in this world,
Accepted in this world as me,
Not as weird,
Just as me!

Jemma Webster (10)
Prestonfield Primary School, Edinburgh

What Did I Do?

What did I do
To deserve not to walk?
I was sitting in the car
And, eh, whoops,
My legs got caught
And crushed.

People in the street
Just ignore me now
And talk to the person
That's pushing me.

Why do they not talk to me?

Just because I'm in a wheelchair
It doesn't mean I can't talk.

I know my legs are all wonky,
And my feet are all squint,
But why does hardly anyone
Talk to me?

Michelle Hannah (10)
Prestonfield Primary School, Edinburgh

Being Blind

Sometimes I hate my life.
All people do is laugh.
I hate it.

People always talk
About the one thing
I can't do,
Not the thousands of things
I can do!

I *can* sing,
I *can* dance,
I *can* talk,
I *can* swim,
I *can* hear,
I *can* read.

I can do all these things
And much more
I just wish people would notice
My achievements.

Brooke Sheridan (10)
Prestonfield Primary School, Edinburgh

Blind

Everyone ignores me,
It's like I'm not there.
I am here!
I'm the one who's meant not to see.
I start to wonder
If I'm really not there.

I can do everything other people do
Except see the world.
I can read,
I can work,
I can play,
I can listen,
I can taste,
I can touch,
But often I get left out,
Ignored.

Oh how I wish they would understand.
All I want to do is tell them
I am able.

Alan Sutherland (10)
Prestonfield Primary School, Edinburgh

I'm Just Me!

I can do anything you can do.
I'm deaf.
So?
That does not matter.

I can run
I can talk
I can use sign language
Read . . . your . . . lips.

You can't, can you?
It seems to me that
You're the disabled one -
I can do two things
You can't do.

Why do people see me
As being disabled?
Why don't they see me
As being *me!*

James Griffin (10)
Prestonfield Primary School, Edinburgh

Blind

Some people say I am blind like a bat,
But I am just the same
As everyone else.
Please someone help me . . .
It makes me upset
When I hear people talk about *me.*

How is it that I am blind
And some people think that's funny?
I can
Write
Play
Think
Talk
And do nearly everything else
That you can.
I am just the same as you,
I am able.

Please just treat me like a person,
Not some kind of monster.
I might not see you,
But I can do the same as you.
There's only one thing wrong with me,
Just my eyes,
It hasn't changed *me.*

Megan McGill (10)
Prestonfield Primary School, Edinburgh

Happiness

Pink is the colour of happiness,
The feeling is so great
When you are going to a fabulous disco party,
But then hate it when you are late;

Getting all dressed up,
And your hair is just about right
Fixing all your make-up,
Because you're gonna be queen tonight;

One last look in the mirror,
And feeling absolutely fine,
Quickly grabbing your handbag,
'Cause the clock has just struck nine.;

Rushing into the car,
And getting ready to go
Checking you've got your lippy,
And off we zoom, *wahoo!*

Cara Robinson (11)
Quarter Primary School, Hamilton

Plasticine

Squishy, squashy
Kind of goo . . .
Stretch it, squash it,
Mould it too.

Build it up, crush it down,
Move it about
And bash it around.

Make a man, make a snail,
Make a plane, even a Great Dane.
It is fun but weighs a tonne.
It's plasticine!

Jack Douglas (10)
Quarter Primary School, Hamilton

The Shadow Man

At night as I climb the stair
I tell myself there's no one there.

But what if there is?
What if he's there?
The shadow man at the top of the stair?
I tell myself there's no one there.

But what if there is? What if he's there?
The shadow man at the top of the stair?
What if he is lurking there in the gloom?
Maybe outside my lovely room.

At night as I climb the stair
I tell myself there's no one there.

Ross Borland (10)
Quarter Primary School, Hamilton

Fear

Fear is nothing
If you're a boy like me
Blood and guts are not scary to me.

But sometimes things like soggy food
I find really disgusting
A bit like my dad's foot.

One more thing that I find disgusting
Is pizza with lots of tomato dressing
Over all my tasty cheese.

Like I said, fear is nothing if you're a boy like me,
Nothing at all really scares me.

Scott Murray (11)
Quarter Primary School, Hamilton

Water

Water can flow, crash and go splash.
It can drip, swirl and whirl.
Water leaks, gushes, roars and splashes.

Water can get through the tiniest cracks,
And can even dribble down people's backs.

Water is sleek, water is smooth,
Water can calm, water can soothe.

Water can freeze, water can boil,
Water can contaminate, water can spoil.

It is swift, strong and agile,
It can go on for mile after mile.

It can be fast, it can be slow,
Its ingredient is H_2O.

Calum Anderson (10)
Quarter Primary School, Hamilton

Ice Cream

I love ice cream all nice and shiny.
Out of Mr Whippy it's the best
With a nice strawberry, chocolate and lemon zest.
Mr Whippy sells lots of things, crisps, juice and candyfloss.
Equis is the second best,
Their raspberry ripple is delicious with a big chunky flake.
It's great.
I sometimes get it from Marinis and Fiondas.
I just *love* ice cream.

Matthew Baird (10)
Quarter Primary School, Hamilton

Shadows

Lying in my bed
I see the *shadow*.

It moves so swiftly,
Like an eagle waiting to nosedive,
To catch its prey.

The *shadow* can bend like nothing I have ever seen before,
It can bend around cupboards, toys, and sneak through the doors.

The *shadow* can take any shape or form,
Big or small, thick or thin, wriggly or straight.

John Rankin (10)
Quarter Primary School, Hamilton

Scruffy

Scruffy is funny
cuddly and sweet
running along beside my feet.
Up and down the
road she goes with
her fluffy white
tail wagging up and down.
Fluffy and white
sometimes is
scruffy.
Forever Scruffy
and I will be the
best friends ever.
You will never
separate me and
my dog, Scruffy.
I love Scruffy.

Kaitlin Young (11)
Quarter Primary School, Hamilton

Summer

When it is summer my friends and I have fun,
Playing in the warm sand and lying in the sun.
We swim in the cold water and dive over the waves
And if we feel very brave we go and explore the caves.
I love running up the sand dunes and sliding down the other side
And when my friends come looking for me I sometimes try to hide.
My sister and I love collecting a variety of shells
And when we string them together they tinkle like little bells.

We also have lots of fun in the autumn
When the leaves are falling on the ground.
My friends and I run through them
And they make a crunchy sound.

Colette Webster
Rayne North School, Inverurie

Dara's Poem

Gymnastics are fantastic,
Netball coaching is quite cool,
School can sometimes be good fun
Like when we use the swimming pool.

There are lots of things I like to do,
Playing with my friends is cool,
Bike rides and trampolining too,
But it's Mum's egg sandwiches that *rule*.

Dara Coull (9)
Rayne North School, Inverurie

My Cat

I have a cat called Blobby,
He will slide along the floor.
Before you can catch hold of him
He will bash into the door.

We love him very much,
He has got a great loud purr.
He is really quite a touch,
He has got black and white fur.

He is only five months old,
I can't take him into school.
The children would like to laugh and play.
He is really not that bold.

Erin Boucher (10)
Rayne North School, Inverurie

My House

My house has three bedrooms,
Two upstairs, one down,
Lit by sash dormers
That slide, I have found.

Downstairs, a bay window,
Big as can be,
Every day I look out
At all I can see.

Alasdair Grant (10)
Rayne North School, Inverurie

Spring Days

Spring is when the blossoms grow,
Plants and flowers bloom,
Roses are the sweetest smell
In indigo and blue.
Never have I seen a day when the sky's so bright,
Grass is growing green again, the perfect day has come.

Daffodils and daisies are dancing all around,
Apricots and apples are growing in the sun,
Yellow, pink and purple are the colours that I see,
Spring is a happy time for you and me.

Mhairi Cruickshank (11)
Rayne North School, Inverurie

Winter

Winter comes every year,
everybody likes it, it makes them cheer.
Nobody hates it, I hope not
because if I did
I'd miss the snow.

Winter sledging, winter slides,
all such fun at Christmas time.
Sledging, sliding every week,
making snowmen - 3 feet.
All such fun, all so great,
have a happy Christmas Day.

Isla Cruickshank (9)
Rayne North School, Inverurie

Autumn

I see the fruit,
It is like someone has bitten into it
And it is lying, rotting away.
You see the conkers just lying on the ground.
Some are jaggy, some are brown and shiny.
I see the water pouring down,
It is like flags are blowing really hard.

You hear the crunching of the leaves,
When you stand on them they rustle and crunch.
I can hear the wind whistling,
It sounds like someone is blowing a whistle.
You can hear the leaves blowing in the background.

I smell the burning of the bonfire,
You smell the burning leaves and the smoke,
I smell the dampness of burning leaves and the smoke.
I smell the dampness of the morning dew.
I touch the frost, it is really chilly.
I had to put on my gloves
Because I didn't want frostbite.

Ashley McDougall (11)
Rigside Primary School, Rigside

Autumn

I see red berries on the trees.
They are soft.
They brighten the trees.
The birds fly in to eat the berries.
I see a bunch of leaves.
I see the conkers fall off the trees.
I hear the leaves crunching.
I hear the leaves falling off the trees.
I smell the fire.
I smell the leaves.
I can smell flowers.
I see the butterflies.

Shanell Norman (9)
Rigside Primary School, Rigside

Autumn

I see the trees full of green and brown leaves.
The apples are growing, I lick my lips,
They look so delicious.
The leaves are falling gently as snow
The flowers are growing and the scent of roses is coming in the air.

I hear the leaves on the fire crackling away
And the conkers are dropping.
I smell the burning leaves, I smell the smoke.
I smell the amber on the trees.

I touch the leaves while walking through them.
I touch the sticky amber on the trees.
When the conkers are ready I go and pick some
And play conkers with my family.
I love autumn.

Martin Ritchie (11)
Rigside Primary School, Rigside

Autumn

I see all the fruit.
I see all the colours in the sky.
I see fruit that is squashed.
I see some green apples on the trees.

I hear the leaves falling from the trees.
I hear the leaves crunching.
I can hear flapping birds.
I can hear the leaves crackling.

I can smell burning leaves.
I can smell smoke.
I can touch snow.
I can touch apples and fruit.

Glen Johnstone (11)
Rigside Primary School, Rigside

Autumn

Here I am, small and invisible,
No one can see me in this sea of colours.
I look high in the sky above the frosted canopy
And see the birds flying south to migrate.
I look down to the ground to see my feet, covered in sparkly fruits.
A gust of wind blows me into a spiky conker tree
                                    full of frost and leaves.

I hear rustling as animals hide under logs and leaves.
I walk faster and faster as the wind gets cold.
I also hear crackling of the fires near me.
I hear the wind howling through the trees.

I smell gunpowder from the fireworks and smoky bonfires too.
I smell mucky leaves going up in flames.
I can feel the cold, frosty wind freezing my wings and my little toes.
I feel sticky from the squished fruit and mud.

Donna Sim (11)
Rigside Primary School, Rigside

It's Autumn

I look up into the sky to see the leaves floating down
like thoughts drifting through my mind.
The colourful leaves blend in with my big, bushy tail
and tickle my long, pointy nose.
The fruit is hanging from the branches ready to eat.
It has been a lovely harvest.
As I walk on the leaves with my four red paws
it's as if I'm crunching lots of nuts.

The sound of the birds swishing through the trees
is like a roller coaster swooshing past my ears
and I love the noise of the crispy frost
lying on the autumn ground.

The feeling of my hands is like the touch of two ice cubes
and the smell of the burning leaves is horrible.

Stephanie Forrest (11)
Rigside Primary School, Rigside

Autumn

I can see children wearing scarves
I can see children wearing bobbly hats
I can see leaves of yellow and brown
And berries too poisonous to eat
But not for animals.
I see cows going off to be milked
And sheep off to market.
I see frost.

I can hear tree branches falling
Chainsaws cutting down the trees
Children screaming in the leaves
Car tyres swishing through the puddles
I can smell school dinners cooking.

Ashley Wynn (11)
Rigside Primary School, Rigside

Autumn

I look up at the tall trees,
I see the colourful leaves fall,
Slowly to the ground,
Swishing side to side like the wind.
I see the birds migrate to the south
To get the warm weather.

I hear the children laughing
And I hear the leaves crunching
When they stand on them.
I hear the birds flapping their wings
Up in the sky.

I smell the burning leaves in the bonfires.
I smell the rot of the fruit.
I touch the wet grass because of the frost.
I touch the spiky conkers
When they are lying on the ground.

Natalie McDougall (11)
Rigside Primary School, Rigside

Autumn

I look up and stare around,
The leaves are drifting down from the trees
And I am thinking it is autumn now.
I see the brown and red leaves
Swooping around as the wind blows a gale.

When I move my small feet one by one
I can hear the crunching of the leaves as I step on them.
I hear the wind whistling
As a flock of birds pass me by.

I smell the rotten fruit as it lies on the cold ground.
I can smell the leaves burning
And the smoke which is circling me now.
I bend down and pick up a conker, it is jaggy.
I feel the spikes as I move the conker around in my hand.

Chloe Freeman (11)
Rigside Primary School, Rigside

Autumn

I see nice brown leaves in the trees and on the ground
And I see all the farmers harvesting the crops.
I can see the beautiful conkers shining in the sunlight.

I can hear the cracking leaves.
I can hear the leaves crackling on the bonfire.
I can hear leaves dropping on the ground.

I can smell the burning of the leaves on the bonfire.
I can smell the damp autumn air when it starts to get cold.

I can touch the cold, cold frost.
I can touch the damp leaves.
I can touch the rotten fruits.

Jenna Blair (11)
Rigside Primary School, Rigside

Autumn

I see the bee in the flower.
I see the burning leaves in the backyards.
I see the brown, hard conkers in spiky shells.
I see the children running through the colourful leaves.
I see the fresh fruit on the trees,
But the rotten fruit on the ground.

I hear the people whistling down the cold street.
I hear the rustling leaves that fell off the tyres.
I hear the leaves getting stood on.
I hear leaves drifting down the chilly street.
I hear the fruit falling from the trees.

I smell burning leaves in the backyard.
I smell damp pavements.
I smell the rotten fruit lying on the cold ground.
I smell the toffee apples on the stalls.

I touch the cracking leaves from the ground.
I touch the sticky trees with sap on them.
I touch the spiky conkers.
I touch the hard, cold ground.

Cory Laird
Rigside Primary School, Rigside

Happiness

Happiness is like a little white puppy
It sounds like a singing bird
It tastes like the biggest chocolate bar
It looks like a roasting hot sun
It feels like my cuddly teddy.

Rhiannon Gage (9)
Rigside Primary School, Rigside

An Autumn's Gift

When I slowly tilted my head up to the trees
I saw the glistening on the branches
And the light coming through them
Shining on the frost that lay on the ground.
The leaves are floating down from the trees
Like thoughts going through my mind.

The crunching of leaves makes me shiver
As I listen to the wind whistling through the forest,
Blowing everything in its path
Like a hurricane going through a village.
I can hear the birds singing sweetly in the sky.

I can almost smell the dampness
That the shower of rain had left on the ground
From the night before.
I feel the jaggy conkers upon layers of mud
And leaves under my feet
As I walk deeper and deeper into the silent woods.

Samantha Dickson (11)
Rigside Primary School, Rigside

Happiness

Happiness is like a beautiful sun.
It sounds like a lovely little puppy crying.
It tastes like yummy fairy cakes.
It smells like a fantastic flower.
It looks like a big chocolate cake.
It feels like a cuddly cat.

Eilidh MacLeod (8)
Rigside Primary School, Rigside

Love

Love is pink like a love heart.
It sounds like a harp.
It tastes like chocolate.
It smells like perfume.
It looks like sparkling roses.
It feels like a big hug.

Stephanie Dickson (8)
Rigside Primary School, Rigside

Happiness

Happiness is yellow like warm sunshine.
It sounds like birds singing outside your bedroom window.
It tastes like the biggest chocolate cake in the world.
It smells like a sweet flower in your garden.
It looks like a sandy beach.
It feels like cuddly bed covers.

Caitlin Cochrane (8)
Rigside Primary School, Rigside

Cheerfulness

Cheerfulness is pink like a love heart.
It sounds like balloons popping.
It tastes like a big chocolate cake.
It sounds like birds singing.
It looks like a beautiful rose.
It feels like a cuddly teddy.

Shannon Kennedy (9)
Rigside Primary School, Rigside

I Wish

I wish, I wish that I were a fish
to swim all day with only some things to play.
I wish that I were a pop star
and have lots of cash, cars and toys that make lots of noise.
I wish that I was a dish
and rubbed around and around and hardly made a sound.
The last wish that I would make . . .
is to take the biggest trip around the world in a hundred days.
I would laze.

Dale Elder (10)
Rosewell Primary School, Rosewell

Una

Una helps me when I'm stuck,
When I fall she cleans me up.

She is really kind and helpful
And always cheerful.

She works hard at her job,
Is confident and capable.

Has worked with many a school teacher
Is very good to Mrs Souter.

Jade Ramsay (9)
Rosewell Primary School, Rosewell

Day Of Honour

He took a deep breath and saw blood from the room ahead,
                                        pouring under the door,
Then he kicked it down and pulled the trigger whilst running,
He jumped, rolled and broke through the passage,
Hid and then threw in a grenade,
The last of the trapped men flew out and got in the truck,
He followed.
He was my grandfather.

Euan Hamilton (11)
Rosewell Primary School, Rosewell

The Bridge

On a murky, misty bridge
My uncle risked his life
To save the souls of British troops.
So on the bridge he stood with a Bren gun in hand.
He pulled the trigger and let lead fly.

He stood there shooting German troops
Waiting for back-up to come.
It was around 20 against 1.
He had to stay collected for the lives of many people.
Soon the back-up came and he was safe.
He was a hero in the eyes of many.

Conner McConnell (11)
Rosewell Primary School, Rosewell

Mrs Hogg

M rs Hogg has a dog called Belle
R eally loves to come to school
S its at her computer doing things for Mrs Souter.

H er happy smiling face
O h how she cheers us all up
G reat to talk to
G reat to work with and that is who she is.

Brian Turnbull (10)
Rosewell Primary School, Rosewell

Mrs Hogg

M y good friend Mrs Hogg
R uns up the halls at top speed.
S peedy as a cat she is.

H ogg is her second name.
O h she is good to me.
G reat to talk to.
G ot to come to school and see her happy face.

Joshua Blair (11)
Rosewell Primary School, Rosewell

Homework

H omework I really hate.
O ne time I even needed my mate.
M y it is a pest.
E ven looking at a bird would be better.
W hen I finish I watch the telly.
O h how I wish I didn't have to do it.
R idiculous I think it is.
K indly don't give me any.

Stuart Easton (10)
Rosewell Primary School, Rosewell

My Best Friend

M y best friend is called Cara.
Y ou can call her Caramel

B ecause she likes that name.
E verywhere she goes
S he is kind and gentle
T o everyone she meets.

F ir trees bow to her
R eindeer gallop around her
I for one like her
E verything about her
N ever will we stop being friends
D eep down I know that.

Victoria Somerville (9)
St Aidan's Primary School, Wishaw

Spain

I love going to Spain,
But the heat is sometimes a pain.
I have been to Majorca, a Spanish island,
I've been to Malaga on the Spanish mainland.

In Alcudia, Majorca there was a super water park,
In Malaga, a castle, built when ages were dark.
There was also mini golf in a Fuengirola resort
Or get hair braids on the beach at C'an Picafort.

I am going back to lovely Spain
And I'll develop Spanish in my brain,
I will be there in the October week,
Spanish I shall speak.

Julie Dobbin (10)
St Aidan's Primary School, Wishaw

Fun Fun Fun

F un makes you feel happy.
U nhappiness is bad,
N o fun makes you feel really, really sad.

F un is playing outside,
U 're playing with your friends,
N o one is unhappy, they're having fun that never ends.

F un isn't being stuck inside
U nenjoyment says indoors
N o sign of happiness just still and unmoving on the floor.

    The key to having fun is quite simple you see,
    You just have to have a friend who is full of glee,
    So just have *fun!*

Gemma Buick (11)
St Aidan's Primary School, Wishaw

Lauren's Hobbies

I like dancing,
I keep fit,
I like singing,
What? It doesn't matter a bit.

I like shopping,
Especially in East Kilbride,
My mum comes with me
So I can decide.

I like chatting,
Especially with my friends
And when we're hanging out
We always talk about jewels and jems!

Lauren Smith (9)
St Aidan's Primary School, Wishaw

Melissa

M y big sister is called Melissa.
E vil sometimes but mostly quite nice.
L ovely girl the teachers say.
I do like Melissa being my sister
S hort brown hair but mostly dyed
S o that's her hair colour.
A bout her face, freckles, blue eyes
 and the same shape as me.

Daniela Clare (9)
St Aidan's Primary School, Wishaw

Happiness

Happiness is yellow like the shining sun.
It looks like newborn lambs lying beside the long grass.
It sounds like soft music in the distance.
Happiness tastes like a freshly baked cake from the oven.
It reminds me of soft cuddly toys.
Happiness feels like the golden sunset shining over the blue water.

Maria Hainey
St Aidan's Primary School, Wishaw

Happiness

Happiness is green like grass in the garden.
It looks like happy people in a smiley bag.
It sounds like children playing at home.
Happiness tastes like sugary, minty sweets.
It reminds me of my team beating their rivals.
Happiness feels like I'm beginning to get rich.

Aidan Dobbin (10)
St Aidan's Primary School, Wishaw

The Man And The Whale

There was a man who liked to sail
His ship was sunk by a whale,
The whale did a flip,
To land on the ship,
And that was the end of his sail.

The man swam so fast,
But not like a blast,
He swam ashore,
After that he was sore,
No sailing for him anymore.

He told his wife,
To get a knife,
'A big one I need,
That whale is going to bleed.'
'Don't be silly' she said,
'Just get to your bed!'

Michael Carroll (10)
St Aidan's Primary School, Wishaw

Kids

Kids are mad
But they're not bad,
Kids are cool
Some like school.

Kids love to play
Some in a rough way,
Some kids play football
Others are very tall.

Kids like to run
And have so much fun,
Some kids are pests
Others are good at tests.

Ryan McCready (10)
St Aidan's Primary School, Wishaw

Global Warming

It's important how we live our lives today,
Because global warming is on its way,
If you go to school in a car, why not walk?
On the way you can talk.
For every bit of litter that you drop,
Some of our ozone layer will pop.
Our weather will go haywire,
Please listen I'm not a liar,
Don't cut down trees,
Try to save little bees,
Plant some more flowers,
Do we really need more towers?
Recycle as much as you can,
Or it may be the end of man.
Stop all these bad gases
Before the Earth's lifetime passes,
What about every creature?
In fact what about all of nature?
I hope you'll have a think,
Before the ozone layer shrinks.

Clare Pearson (11)
St Aidan's Primary School, Wishaw

Friends

F riends are fab
R eal good fun
I 'm best friends with
E rin, she's my pal,
N o one's like her,
D ear me no,
S o to end I will say.

Friends are fab!

Amy Cassidy (9)
St Aidan's Primary School, Wishaw

Spooky House

Is that a spooky house I see?
Right next to that big old tree,
There's a smelly bat,
And a battered cat.

Let's go inside,
For a very spooky ride,
There's a mummy,
She looks crummy.

There's a ghost,
It scares me most,
He is chasing after me,
I try to find a key.

There's the door,
There's no more,
So that's the end of that.

Emma Hay (11)
St Aidan's Primary School, Wishaw

Bones

Bones, bones, bones, bones,
Rattling, shaking, near your bed.
You wish you were dead,
Because of all these bones.

Bones, bones, troublesome things,
Birds have them in their wings,
You can get them broken,
Get them soaken.

Ha! Ha! They're OK,
It's hard for them to break or fray,
So remember, we've got them either way.

Nicolas Friskey (11)
St Aidan's Primary School, Wishaw

A Special Night

There's nothing quite like European nights,
The singing, the dancing, the crowds, the frights,
The atmosphere sensational, the condition's great,
But the real question is - will we remember this date?
The skill of the football is there to be seen,
Will we be a good enough team?
1-0 at half-time - not looking so good,
A penalty save put us back in the mood,
A quick breakaway across from the right,
Gave us a goal to remember that night,
Then a special man came on,
Right in the middle of one of our songs,
We lost 3-1 a lot of tearful sights,
But there's still nothing quite like
European nights.

Sophie McGinness (11)
St Aidan's Primary School, Wishaw

Once Upon A Rhyme

Once upon a rhyme
There was a very special time,
It was about Cinderella,
She got her fella,
It was also about Humpty Dumpty,
He was a bit of a numpty,
He tumbled off the wall,
With a great big fall,
It was also about Jack and Jill,
They fell down the hill.
They had to go up again,
For when they fell,
The water went down the drain,
This was my special rhyme,
That happened once upon a time.

Francesca Campbell (10)
St Aidan's Primary School, Wishaw

School

I like school
Because it's cool
But still you need to abide by the rules,
My teacher's Mrs Feeney
And she's really good
She teaches like a teacher should.

She gives us maths, writing and spelling,
Mrs Feeney does this without any yelling,
In PE, we do basketball,
Watch you don't stumble or you will fall,
We do French, we're learning,
Environmental studies is also swell.

Art is fun,
In PE you can run,
Playtime's the best,
It's a chance for you to rest
And when it's time to eat your lunch
Everybody can munch, munch, munch!

Christopher McKeown (10)
St Aidan's Primary School, Wishaw

The Great Eagle

The great eagle
Flying through the night
Next to the seagull
Its prey is in sight.

The great eagle
Flying over height
Its prey almost invisible
It will give it a fright.

The great eagle
Its eyes on its prey
The great eagle in the night
The prey was eaten just in one bite!

Joseph Miller (10)
St Aidan's Primary School, Wishaw

Alphabet Places

A merica is a brilliant place,
B elgium is where I lost my brace,
C aribbean is really hot,
D enmark I'd go to on the trot,
E ngland has a long history,
F rance has things that are a mystery,
G ermany started a world war,
H olland I found out about the minataur,
I reland I wouldn't give it an ace,
J amaica hasn't a lot of space,
K enya has animals running wild,
L yon in the winter is quite mild,
M anchester has a football team,
N etherlands strip is an orange dream,
O xford there is a uni there,
P ortugal transports a lot of pears,
Q ueensland is in Australia's land,
R ussia has indeed no sand,
S pain has a red and yellow flag,
T urkey, I found the heat a drag,
U kraine I don't know a lot about,
V ietnam I'll give it the benefit of the doubt,
W ales is where you work as a team,
X anadu is just a dream,
Y ork I've never been to,
Z ambia was where I saw funny animals in the zoo.

Kyle Neilly (10)
St Aidan's Primary School, Wishaw

In My House

In my house, there's six,
We laugh, we cry, we have fun,
I play the keyboard,
Everyone else listens,
They all clap when I'm finished.

Jennifer Dyer (10)
St Aidan's Primary School, Wishaw

The Big Fat Cat

I have a pet cat
Who is so, so fat
He eats all day
My cat will never play.

We gave him healthy cat food
But he just went in a mood
We didn't have a clue
What to do!

We went to the vet
Because he's my only pet
He lost some weight
Now he can slip under the gate.

Caitlin Foley (11)
St Aidan's Primary School, Wishaw

Transport

I used to come home on the bus
But it became too much of a fuss,
So I went in the car
But my mum got stuck in thick, black tar.

Then I took a taxi
And the driver's name was Maxi,
I also went on a plane
But that crashed into a train.

Truly! I went on a train
But never again the driver was insane,
Finally I went on a bike
And eventually found something I like!

Michael Donnelly (11)
St Aidan's Primary School, Wishaw

The Giant

There once was a giant from New Zealand
Who had a very funny feeling
He rolled on his back
And jumped up like that!
And his head bounced right off the ceiling.

Daniel Gaffney (11)
St Aidan's Primary School, Wishaw

Bubbles

The bubbles in streams
Bursting as they tumble on
Laughing as they go.

Darren Dobbin (11)
St Aidan's Primary School, Wishaw

Dragon - Haiku

Oh flying dragon
Breathing smoky fireballs through
Your mouth, blazing bright.

Andrew McCluskey (10)
St Aidan's Primary School, Wishaw

Footballs

Football is a funny thing to play,
I do it nearly every day,
Scoring goals between the poles
Winning teams is a dream
4-0 is a thrill.

Josh McPhail (10)
St Aidan's Primary School, Wishaw

My Best Friend

M y best friend is called Josh McPhail
Y ou are always there for me

B efore I came here, I had no friends
E ventually, I made one and that was you
S porty and kind you are too
T ogether we make great friends.

F orever friends we will be
R ace like runners we will be
I will cherish our friendship
E very time I am sad, you make me laugh
N ow every day you are sad, I'll make you happy just like that
D eep down underneath you will be my friend always.

Cara McQuade (9)
St Aidan's Primary School, Wishaw

Going On Holiday

I'm going on holiday
This will be fun
I'm going to Oasis
To buy a big fat bun.

I'm going to go swimming
And go down a flume
And when the waves come on
I'll go and make them boom.

I will go and hire a bike
And cycle to the country club
I will climb on the climbing wall
Then play a game of football.

Then we will drive home
And go to sleep in the car
Then when we get home
My dad will play his guitar.

Paul McCafferty (9)
St Aidan's Primary School, Wishaw

Things I Like

Here are some of the things I like
Maybe 1, 2 or 3,
I like swimming because it is fun
In the summer I got in *free*.

I like cycling all around the street
It is very exciting
The wind blows you from side to side
So it's best if you stay on your seat.

I like singing because it has a beat
Sometimes it has a lovely tune
It's better if you sing along
Then you can tap your feet.

This is all I have to say
Please excuse me . . .
Because I am going out to play.

Chloe Archer (9)
St Aidan's Primary School, Wishaw

Tulips

Tulips are my favourite flowers
They have a lovely smell
And every time I have a cold,
The tulips make me well.

Whenever I feel let down
Or I'm in a bad mood,
I talk to one of the tulips
And it makes me feel good.

I love the little tulips
As they grow and grow and grow
And every time I water them,
The wind blows and they give a little flow.

I love my tulips.

Katrina Mitchell (9)
St Aidan's Primary School, Wishaw

Birthdays

B irthdays are great days
I just love it when it's mine
R ip open presents
T he cake is waiting to be cut
H appy Birthday is sung
D ad has got the day off work
A big present's waiting in the morning
Y ou must love it when it's your birthday.

Joseph Devine (10)
St Aidan's Primary School, Wishaw

My Mummy

M is for Mum
Y is for you

M is for magical
U is for understanding
M is for marvellous
M is for merry
Y is for yummy Mummy!

Emma McAlinden (10)
St Aidan's Primary School, Wishaw

Football

Football is great to play
Everyone can do it even the girls say
Kick the ball about
Then score a goal and everyone will shout
'Good goal!'
Football is a good exercise
Everyone has to work in a team
Not to be nasty and mean.

Danny Cooper (10)
St Aidan's Primary School, Wishaw

My Best Friend

My best friend in the world is Clare,
She is terrified of big, brown bears,
She's in the choir, and excellent at singing,
She likes tennis and swimming.

Clare likes to climb high trees,
She absolutely hates bees,
She likes hamsters and cats,
Her attic is full of scary black bats.

Clare is really, really cool,
She is in high school,
Clare has got a really cool trend,
She is my very best friend.

Alexandra Devlin (11)
St Aidan's Primary School, Wishaw

Football

Celtic is a football team
Some of the fans are really keen
Celtic are, to me, the best
They are better than all the rest.

Real are a team from Spain
When they're hurt, they're in pain
Man Utd also are very good
So is the crowd when they're in a good mood.

Football is a great game
Most of the players have honour and fame
All the teams work hard to score
Although the fans all shout for more.

Stephen Collins (11)
St Aidan's Primary School, Wishaw

Happiness

Happiness is green like the football grass,
It looks like the ball in the back of the net,
It sounds like the cheers in the crowd,
Happiness tastes like refreshing lemonade in the sun,
It reminds me of when my team wins 1 - 0,
Happiness feels like the great cheer after the great game.

Cameron McCann (10)
St Aidan's Primary School, Wishaw

My Family

M y family are good to me
Y ummy dinners they make for me.

F amilies are the best things to have
A ll of my family love me
M ums are great to have to take care of you
I love my family
L ucky I am to have a family
Y ou are great - my family.

Lorraine Gillies (9)
St Aidan's Primary School, Wishaw

Best Friend

My friend and I do lots of things
That we enjoy together
If I am sad she makes me happy
By cheering me up,
If we fall out we are sad,
But glad when we fall in again
As we are best friends.

Megan Molloy (9)
St Aidan's Primary School, Wishaw

Animals

A nimals can be pets
N eeding to be taken to the vet's
I t's hard work having pets
M ostly there's no regrets
A nimals can be lots of fun
L ovely when they play and run
S o look after your pets and they may
             not need to go to the vet's.

Erin Baxter (9)
St Aidan's Primary School, Wishaw

School

S chool's great!
C lass work is great!
H omework's great!
O h, so good!
O h, so great!
L aughing with your mates.

Leigh Jarvie (10)
St Aidan's Primary School, Wishaw

Juice

J uice it's so scrummy, you can't resist it,
U ltimately the best,
I would drink juice all day if I could,
C ome on have some juice,
E specially brilliant when it's cold.

Luke Terence William Scott (10)
St Aidan's Primary School, Wishaw

Doing Things

Football is a hobby,
Then I'll go to the lobby,
To see Molly,
After I have a lolly,
The next day,
I'll lay
Then my mum will say, 'Go out to play!'
And there's Fay,
I go to sleep,
Then I leap
And keep in touch with friends.

David McCulloch (10)
St Aidan's Primary School, Wishaw

Football

Football is great, football is fun,
It was great when it begun,
All the girls wanted to play
But the boys just said, 'No way!'
4-0 will they come back?
Will they come out with a smashing crack?
4-4 what a game hope the next will be the same!

Kevin McGhee (9)
St Aidan's Primary School, Wishaw

Grass Haiku

Grass is soft and smooth,
It is green and looks so nice
Smells so fresh when cut.

James McKenna (10)
St Aidan's Primary School, Wishaw

Springtime - Haiku

I like spring, it's fun
New baby lambs being born
Gamboling in fields.

Paul Hainey (11)
St Aidan's Primary School, Wishaw

Snowdrops - Haiku

The snowdrops in spring
Dancing in the chilly breeze
Beautiful and white.

Jade Clark (11)
St Aidan's Primary School, Wishaw

A Globe

Looking down I saw
The sea, the land and lots more
Lots of animals
Lots of adults and children
How did just God make the Earth?

Ashleigh Bannatyne (11)
St Aidan's Primary School, Wishaw

The Owl

The owl sang hoot hoot
Flying through the stormy night
To find some shelter
The wind started loud howling
And the trees began to sway.

Kathleen Delaney (10)
St Aidan's Primary School, Wishaw

Victorian Times

In Victorian times, Victoria was the queen,
When her husband died, she could not be seen,
She had lots of children, they are not alive today,
But when you think about it you'd wish they had stayed,
To tell us about the things back then,
Like when they didn't discover the pen,
When Albert died, Victoria wore black,
Quite frankly I think she should not look back on her reign,
Or on the things that gave her pain.

Cameron Martin (10)
St Patrick's Primary School, Motherwell

Oh How I Wish

The three Musketeers they have big ears,
They have long hair, they have red coats,
But they look more like billy goats.

They fight with swords all day and night,
Beware my men, you'll get a fright,
They right the wrong, as they go along,
Beware my men, they are mighty strong.

On horses they ride, side by side,
Oh what a sight to see!
Oh I wish it was me.

Jack Sweeney (8)
St Patrick's Primary School, Motherwell

Winter

W ooly jumpers, scarves and hats,
 I n the house everyone freezing,
N o more sun or hot days,
T orrential storms in the night,
E nding with snow on the ground,
R udolph the reindeer comes in winter.

Julia McKendrick (8)
St Patrick's Primary School, Motherwell

Art

Card and paper, sticky glue,
Art is fun but messy too,
If you are bored with nothing to do,
Art is fun for me and you,
Bits of paper here and there,
Drawing animals, grizzly bears,
Colouring, painting, the fun does not stop,
Draw balloons bursting,
Pop, pop, *pop!*

Lisa Dignall (10)
St Patrick's Primary School, Motherwell

Twinkle

I have a little fairy
At the bottom of my garden.
She's pink and has twinkling wings of snow,
And sometimes she sings,
She's there every morning,
Waiting for me,
To sprinkle all her fairy dust,
To give me a happy day.

Sheryl McCulloch (9)
St Patrick's Primary School, Motherwell

Star

Star, starlight
Who could forget that night,
It shone past the moonlight
Breaking the clouds
And giving light all through the night.

From the tip of its point
To the end of its toes
It shone so bright
With all its might.

Rachael Houston (9)
St Patrick's Primary School, Motherwell

Dolphins And Whales

The sea can be calm, the sea can be rough,
But when the sea is calm, the dolphin comes out to play.

In the moonlight the acrobatic dolphin darts,
Dashes and dives. The dolphin
Does amazing flips with its small tail.

The dolphin's blue silky skin slides through the water,
As it darts through the blue sea,
The dolphin is cute and small,
It has a big relation - the whale.

The big whale is blue and silky too,
It darts and dashes but not as fast as the dolphin,
When the whale breathes it makes an eye-catching fountain.

Catriona Curtis (9)
St Peter's RC Primary School, Aberdeen

Rivers

Rivers shine like the stars at night, glowing like day
Walking round the river makes me jump up high and
Shout out loud and say 'Rivers are fun, rivers live all day long.'
Rivers can flood over the land to destroy all living things,
Rivers, rivers, please don't overflow your water,
We are around the river to gather singing a song,
Good river, goodnight.

Amir Nazari (9)
St Peter's RC Primary School, Aberdeen

Beneath The Sea

Beneath the sea in a dreamland of blue
You'll hear a mermaid calling out for you
A mermaid with a silver crown
You won't ever see this mermaid frown.

Beneath the sea, beyond the deep
It's dark and black and it's quite steep
Beneath the sea in the open wide
There is a dolphin that will try to hide.

The dolphin is a soft kind fellow
He's very gentle and extremely mellow
If you go down beneath the deep blue sea
There's many a miracle to tempt thee.

Maria Giaimis (9)
St Peter's RC Primary School, Aberdeen

My Laughter Poem

My laughter is yellow
It smells like fragrant roses
It feels like a jacuzzi bubbling over me
It looks like a huge yellow smiling face rolling over me
And that is how laughter feels for me!

Matthew Harazim (9)
St Peter's RC Primary School, Aberdeen

The Olympics

The medals round the athlete's neck
Shine in all their glory,
I really like the Olympics.

The five rings stand for the five continents,
So that all of the athletes of the world can play,
I really like the Olympics.

There are lots of games for all the athletes,
My favourites are the gymnastics,
I really like the Olympics.

The Olympics are for everyone,
For you and me to unite everyone
And to have peace and happiness,
I really like the Olympics.

Marina Georgiou (9)
St Peter's RC Primary School, Aberdeen

My Pets

My cat is fat and fluffy,
He is a real 'toughie'
He has a great big tummy
And an evil stare
If you dare to cuddle him!

I have a fish who was gold,
Now she's turning white and old.

I have a catfish who snuffles,
With four whiskers and all his brothers and his sisters.

Hannah Crawford (9)
St Peter's RC Primary School, Aberdeen

Animals

Animals are weird and varied
Skinless, furred or even haired
Fish have scales but not for weighing
And you'll never understand a word they're saying
Beaver's teeth are long and funny
But a walrus' teeth reach down to its tummy
Seagulls' beaks are sharp and pecky
Run when you see one, don't stop for a seccy
Rabbits have big ears made for hearing
They hear anything from a whisper to lots of loud cheering
Croakety croak goes the frog
This causes a growl from the dog
Dolphins are very cute and fun
Go to Florida if you want to swim with one
Animals are just so much fun
There's something there for everyone.

Megan Allan (9)
St Peter's RC Primary School, Aberdeen

Wildlife

Wild is life we would not live without it,
Lions are fast not as fast as cheetahs,
Birds and frogs, worms and logs and
A sheep that said 'Baa.'
Cows go moo and a dog that said 'Boo'
Tiger is striped like a bee.

Sam Donnelly (9)
St Peter's RC Primary School, Aberdeen

Penguins

Penguins are so cute,
They waddle and they wiggle,
They're funny little creatures,
And they really make me giggle.

I like the way they swim
And the way they feed their chicks,
They're always up to something
With their funny little tricks.

It's true that I love penguins
I really, really do
I can't wait until the next time
I see them at the zoo.

Ashlay Manson (8)
St Peter's RC Primary School, Aberdeen

Space

Space is dark,
Space is light,
I like Saturn because it's bright.

Stars are shining,
Shining bright,
I like Saturn because it's light.

Moon is beaming,
Beaming bright,
But I don't care because Saturn is gleaming.

Carrie Hutchison (9)
St Peter's RC Primary School, Aberdeen

Rivers

The water crashed over the rocks,
poured down the mountainside
hitting the bottom of the waterfall
and rushed through the rapids as strong as a bull.

The water roared, pounced like a lion,
rumbling down the rocks,
crashing, bashing, hurling itself down.

Salmon leapt up, trying to leap away
from the gnashing teeth of death.
The water lunged, plunged, swayed
and swished down the mountainside.

Down the mountainside it went gathering rocks with it
and crushing the rocks to pieces.

Jonathan Simpson (11)
South Morningside Primary School, Edinburgh

Flowing Water

F alling, flowing
L ashing, long-suffering
O paque, optical
W indswept, white
I solated, incredible
N eglected, noisy
G leaming, gentle

W hispering, wondering
A ctive, amazing
T eemed, tempered
E nchanting, environmentally friendly
R aging river.

Anna Campbell (11)
South Morningside Primary School, Edinburgh

Flowing Water

Splish, splosh,
Is how a new river goes.
The river is a mysterious force.
Water trampling a path,
developing and spreading over the land masses.

There is no rest for the river.
Smashing, bashing rocks in the floods,
moving them onto the shore.

Calm and cool.
Only causing problems when it is
in the flooding season.
Moving mighty mountains.

Alexander Smith (10)
South Morningside Primary School, Edinburgh

Flowing Water

Raindrops trickle down the mountains,
they form streams in the valleys below.
When some of those streams join up together
they make a river flow.

As that river becomes bigger and bigger,
it tumbles, rumbles down the hills
right through forests into the woods.

It becomes faster, faster,
it sways and splashes, winding its way
through cities and fields.

It becomes slower,
slower as it reaches its end.

Drew Anderson (11)
South Morningside Primary School, Edinburgh

The River Is A Fierce Tiger

As it runs faster and faster down the mountain
it tears away rocks and dirt.

It splashes, bashes against the rocks
and wears them away into nothing but dust.

It brings out its huge claws, places them into the ground
and it leaves a deep claw scar.

The fast-running water reaches and scoops
and throws fish into the air.

The raging water starts thundering, changes into a waterfall
and dives down with a huge *splash!*

As it tumbles down the hillside
it splashes, thrashes and bashes against the rocks.

Its wildness and its power is such
that no one dares to enter.

Megan Forde (11)
South Morningside Primary School, Edinburgh

The River

The river deer rumbles
down through the hills
passing forests full of snow.

His hooves thunder as he leaps high.
He pounds the frothing water,
racing among the fish.

He lowers his giant antlers
as he carves a stone walkway,
throwing aside boulders like a crane.

The river deer slows and widens
like a yawn.
He sleeps silently.
Waking, he turns to the sea
his grazing herd.

Romane Allanson (11)
South Morningside Primary School, Edinburgh

Flowing Water

As fast as a leopard,
as loud as a lion.
Thrashing, smashing, bashing the rocks,
the river is a wild bull,
untamed, unwanted, yet marvelled at.

So strong, so powerful,
no one dares enter
for fear of death or injury.
Although its power is known by all,
some test their luck and pay the price.

Winding, binding, it chooses its prey.
All that stands in its way shall perish.
Finally -
the bull is tamed by a brave matador - the sea.

Calmed, tired, the bull slows down,
lazily grazing on the seabed,
old and withered from the journey.
The river *was* a wild bull.

Michael Faulkner (11)
South Morningside Primary School, Edinburgh

Flowing Water

The water trickling from a crack, just like a dripping tap.
Gently winding, turning, twisting like a snake.
Now it's crashing, tumbling, twirling, spinning,
No longer gentle but strong
Just like a fierce, wild lion roaring, and running
As it plunges into a haze of white froth,
Gushing, pouring in the blue mass, the sea.

Jamie Collier (11)
South Morningside Primary School, Edinburgh

Flowing Water

The river is a book, and when the river gets older a page will turn.

The river is young, it is colourful, lively and loud.
It plays with the darting, wriggling, dashing fish that follow it around.
The gleaming, gushing, rushing contents bubble below the surface,
making it foam.
Small rippling waves roll over the pebbly rocks, making them smooth
and flat.

The river is older, slower, has less energy.
It is deeper, colder, stronger than it was.
The winding river splashes-sploshes, as it rolls over the pebbly ground.
The sun bounces off the crystal-clear water and reflects the trees that
peer over at it.

The river is moaning-groaning as it gently flows over the summit
and races down the mountainside feeling heavy.
The colours that it had are fading.

The river is on its last page.
It is old, slow and out of breath, slowly departing out to sea.
It sings with the wind as it flows.
Suddenly it is there, it is at the sea.

It is now immense and strong, but old.
It smoothes the shells and sand as it crawls over them.
That is the sea.

Alice Dalkin (10)
South Morningside Primary School, Edinburgh

The River

The river is as cold as ice,
gleaming like crystals
in the sunlight.
Rocks tumble from the hillside,
over the edge.
Water creates a waterfall.

Joel Paatelainen (11)
South Morningside Primary School, Edinburgh

Flowing Water

The winding river gushed along, harassing the rocks which lay beyond
Bubbling and flowing steadily, it arrived to see a frothy waterfall and
plunged down its contents, billowing out below.
It smacked upon the water and taking up its courage it carried on,
gleaming like a star as the summer sun reflected upon it.
Splashing along, young at heart, sprinkling water about,
gradually growing wider, sidling towards the sea like a long snake.
Almost silent, the peaceful river hollowed out the land
and only the sound of gurgling could be heard.
Gently twisting, among the rocks and boulders not strong enough
yet to manoeuvre them.
Growing fast, collecting rainfall, its appearance like a sheet of silk
as it flowed towards the sea.
In its path lay a boulder, its power and might and will grew strong
and the almighty river submerged the boulder in its depths.
Surges of energy came shooting out and the boulder rolled on
its side, defeated.
The last few metres to go and like a bolt of lightning the river
increased in speed and with a whoosh of pleasure it shot into the
open sea.

Rhian Hughes (10)
South Morningside Primary School, Edinburgh

Flowing Water

Slowly rolling down the mountain
the river was sliding over the battered rocks.
Gradually picking up speed it scratched
and bashed anything in its way.
Suddenly down, down, *splash!*
It was calm again as it twisted and turned
through the forest, full of life.
Further down the river, the forest people lived their simple lives,
fishing, drinking and washing in the river's warm water.
It got closer and closer to the sea
where it could stretch out finally.

Calum Fergusson (11)
South Morningside Primary School, Edinburgh

Flowing Water

It begins as a trickle,
Water so gentle, so gentle.
But it's strong enough to shape all stones,
All rocks - even hard metal.

Just small amounts of water,
Yet in the end a huge river.
As it travels down and down,
It moves swaying and meandering.

Then at the waterfall, it pushes boulders off.
The water turns into a tremendous force.
As it lands in a big pit,
The sides are covered in moss.

Horace Li (10)
South Morningside Primary School, Edinburgh

Flowing Water

The river is a hungry wolf
a hot-blooded predator
stalking its prey
cautiously and quietly,
with sharp claws and pointy teeth.

At night when the moon is out
and the storm has passed, is when
the predator comes out.
Swirling around quietly and swiftly.
It goes wherever it wants to go
through cracks and open doors
taking over land and wrecking houses.

When morning comes
it settles down.
Flooding the land.
It has had its fill.

Stuart Noble (11)
South Morningside Primary School, Edinburgh

Waterfall

Dancing, prancing,
tumbling, stumbling.
Toppling, rumpling,
shoving and pushing.

Bolting, darting, dashing, flashing,
racing, running.
Hurrying, hurtling, streaking and tearing,
hastening towards the looming roar.

Louder, louder.
Roaring!
Thundering!

Streaks of blue, white and green,
Forcing, jostling,
Foaming and rushing.

Breathtaking, magnificent,
sensational, stunning.

Bewitching, entrancing,
fascinating, enchanting,
mesmerising, enthralling.

A waterfall!

Min Ke (11)
South Morningside Primary School, Edinburgh

Flowing River

The river was as clear as glass,
darker and darker the river was.
As it was flowing down the stream,
it was as fast as lightning.
Whipping through the pathway,
coming down the waterfall.
Splashing, roaring and thrashing
down the waterfall.

Andrew Mackay (11)
South Morningside Primary School, Edinburgh

Raindrops

The raindrops swept down
disturbing the smooth, subtle water.
Splattering, pattering a sweet melody
As down from the sky raindrops flowed.

The raindrops fell down like golf balls
hitting the restful river.
Arguing with the rocks,
moving mighty mountains,
pushing flowing fountains.

Raindrops swelled the swollen river.
Now the river was changed -
dark, menacing, flooding.

Fiona Armstrong (10)
South Morningside Primary School, Edinburgh

Flowing Water

I start as a little trickle,
frolicking down a mountain like a bubbly little lamb,
flipping down the hillside, running across the land.
Like an acrobatic snake, I slither round and round the zigzag path,
picking up speed as other rivers join me.
I am going really strong now, no trickle am I.
I am at my strongest point, knocking down trees, boulders, walls.
Bolting on my way, building force, foaming at the edges and
smoothing rocks.
All my force will die away as I sidle along to the call of the sea.
I am just a peaceful river, withered, tired from the long journey down.
My indulging sounds make people stop and listen
as I tearfully trickle to the big, blue sea.

Leila Marshall (10)
South Morningside Primary School, Edinburgh

The Flowing River

Gurgling, bubbling flowing down
the rocky cliff side.
Rushing, falling, flowing down,
getting bigger as the day goes on.

Older, but still the river
is silently flowing over rock and pool
trying to find the way downhill.
Splashing, rushing over rock and pool,
flowing over steep rock,
spraying, falling, flowing on.

Flowing on, down, down,
on towards the sea.
Slowing down more and more,
going on and on.
Smaller rivers join it
Always flowing on, on,
the sea is beckoning.

Flowing faster, sweeping things aside.
Moving on, on and getting faster by the minute
then it slows down and becomes tired.
It is nothing compared to he bubbling stream that it was.
It is getting slower, slower as it moves on.
The sea is beckoning all the while
The sea is there and welcoming,
urging the river on all the while.
It's there, it's shining all the time
and welcoming the river
that was once a bubbling stream
away up in the mountains.

Night falls and the river has reached the sea.
The river is still
and now everything sleeps
resting, thinking of the long day to come.
The sun rises and the river starts in long day again.

Eleanor Williams (10)
South Morningside Primary School, Edinburgh

The River

A little trickle of water runs down the hillside,
As young as a foal, as gentle as a lamb.
Gurgling slightly as it skips down the valley,
Buttercups swaying gently at its banks.

A small stream runs through the countryside,
As clear as crystal, shiny as gold,
Gathering speed with every metre,
Growing wider all the while.

A fast-flowing river runs around the wood,
Running like a hungry dog after a lamb,
Taking with it strength and courage,
To brave whatever it can.

Strong rapids splutter and splash by the rocks,
Wild horses' hooves galloping fast and free,
With strength to carry many trees
And to let boulders roll free.

A tremendous waterfall crashes down to the ground,
Deer being chased by a fox,
Leaping down over the rocks,
To continue on their way.

A tired-out river runs into the sea,
Sighing as it flows into the salty brine.
Still young at heart it rides the waves,
Knowing that soon it will have to go on its journey once again.

Kirsty Melton (11)
South Morningside Primary School, Edinburgh

What Am I?

I flow, froth and bubble,
Whirl, twirl my way down.
I tumble over jagged rocks but they'll never hurt me.
I like spraying people though they never spray me back.

My surface is usually not broken,
Yet if you watch ripples do appear.
Fish dart, dash, flash, splash then scatter.
Dragonflies hover at the sight of me.

The sun streaming over the horizon
Made my periwinkle-blue shallows shine.
The breeze made my long reeds sway
And the beautiful petals of all the flowers fly away.

I twinkle innocently
At the red 'n' yellow bridges that tower over me.
Overhanging branches fall on top of me,
Flowers bloom on my banks.

When I meet the end of my journey,
Some think it's just begun.
Sorry I have to leave you now
But wait, answer me this:

What am I?

Annie Nicoll Baines (10)
South Morningside Primary School, Edinburgh

The Forgotten River

The young bright river bubbles,
The young bright river flows.
Who knows where the river will go.

The river crashes,
The river pounds,
The river pummels the rocks.

The river is getting old now,
But still it never stops.
It works from dawn till dusk,
It must, it must.

The river slithers down the summit,
Reaching the hungry valley below.
It tumbles, it turns, it yawns and moans,
And how the river groans.

The forgotten river tumbles through the valley,
It's coming to the woods.
It zooms, it splashes, it bashes and crashes
To meet its destination at the old grey crook.

Susie Purvis (11)
South Morningside Primary School, Edinburgh

The River Is A Snake

The river is like a long snake
that flows through the lake.
It swishes and sways
and captures its prey,
as it icicles and tricycles all through the day.
It flushes and slushes
all throughout May.

Kirsti Clark (10)
South Morningside Primary School, Edinburgh

The Spirit Of Water

The river starts deep underground.
Bubbling and bubbling
then bursts out of a hole with a *pound!*
It's a trickle now
it hits the rocks but it doesn't go *pow!*
It widens, ready to crash,
hits the rocks with a *splash!*
Now it's rough
along the bank it goes *scuff!*
Down and down the
water falls
into one huge water pool
the sea.

Jamie Long (11)
South Morningside Primary School, Edinburgh

Darkness

Darkness is pitch-black like a raging storm,
With lightning bolts jumping out of the sky.
It sounds like silence in the dead of night, echoing around my head,
It tastes like dark chocolate, gone off in the fridge,
It feels like spiders, crawling up my back with their hairy legs
and feelers,
It smells like fear of darkness tonight,
It looks like an empty space, deserted with only rotting,
smelling decay,
It reminds me of Hallowe'en and a great lightning storm echoing
in the sky.

Eleanor Chadwick (10)
Springfield Primary School, Linlithgow

Happiness

Happiness is orange, like the summer sun shining.
Reminding me of my friends.
Looking like a world of smiles,
Stretching wide for many miles.
Smelling like the summer.
Feeling like God is with you, keeping you company.
It tastes like your favourite meal,
And it sounds like laughter, pouring further inside your ears.

Conor Cochrane (11)
Springfield Primary School, Linlithgow

Fun

Fun is yellow like the sun
It reminds me of children playing.
It sounds like laughter,
It smells like ice cream running down my hand
It looks like fluffy marshmallows
It feels like kittens
It tastes like chocolate melting in my mouth.

Clair Kirkwood (11)
Springfield Primary School, Linlithgow

Fun

Fun is the luminous colour pink,
Fun smells like a spray of smelly perfume,
Fun feels like a big fluffy pillow that my sister has,
Fun tastes like a big stack of fluffy candyfloss,
Fun looks like a big funny clown with his big shiny red nose,
It reminds me of my big huggable rabbit at home.

Jamie Morrison (11)
Springfield Primary School, Linlithgow

Laughter

Laughter is light blue like the hot afternoon skies
Laughter reminds me of funny jokes
Laughter looks like a clown
Laughter smells like an apple pie
Laughter tastes like sweet strawberries
Laughter sounds like merry chuckling
Laughter feels like a comfy pillow.

Jed Anderson (11)
Springfield Primary School, Linlithgow

Darkness

Darkness is black like a big hairy spider
It tastes like a burnt piece of toast
It reminds me of a dark lane
It smells like rotten cheese
It sounds like echoes in my head
It feels like a hard rock
It looks like the black sky at night.

Sophie Lynch (11)
Springfield Primary School, Linlithgow

Hate

Hate is red like boiling lava
It reminds me of my brother
It tastes like salt water
It sounds like the scream of a terrified human
It looks like a rusty axe
It feels like spikes sticking in you
It smells like a decaying body.

David Silk (11)
Springfield Primary School, Linlithgow

Darkness

Darkness is black like the black spiky railings
standing straight and still
It reminds me of the street without lamps
on at night
It smells like rotten cheese
It looks like a big black hole that never ends
It tastes like something in the back of my throat
It sounds like nothing, just silence
It feels like rats crawling up my spine.

Joanna Graham (11)
Springfield Primary School, Linlithgow

Sadness

Sadness is navy-blue like the deep dark oceans
It sounds like the sobs of a child crying
It tastes like a lump in the back of my throat
It feels like a tear trickling down my face
It looks like lonely people walking the streets at night
It reminds me of the pain of a hospital stay
It smells like burning all through the day.

Joanne Riddell (10)
Springfield Primary School, Linlithgow

Darkness

Darkness is black like a never-ending tunnel going on and on forever,
It tastes like the stillness in a deep dark cave,
It sounds like the silence that echoes in my head,
It smells like a tear running down my face,
It feels like death, never to live,
It looks like nothing, nothing in my head,
It reminds me of blackness that never ends.

Leah Swan (11)
Springfield Primary School, Linlithgow

Hunger

Hunger is brown like a cheeseburger,
It tastes like a piece of chocolate.
It sounds like someone eating,
It smells like frying.
Hunger feels like your stomach, rumbling like a volcano.
Hunger looks like a gaping mouth,
It reminds me of an empty stomach.

Gareth Oliver (10)
Springfield Primary School, Linlithgow

Fun

Fun is green like grass growing,
It smells like flowers that grow in summer,
It tastes like sweets that melt in my mouth,
It looks like the sun that shines all day,
It sounds like laughing in my ear,
It feels like happiness through my body,
It reminds me of playing with my two best friends.

Katie Allison (11)
Springfield Primary School, Linlithgow

Darkness

Darkness is black, black as a dead beating heart,
It sounds like the hysterical laughter of a madman,
It tastes like poison, greed and terror,
It smells like sweat, blood and fear,
It looks like space without any stars,
It feels like a black ball of fire overwhelming me,
It reminds me of a blazing tiger raging at the steel bars
surrounding him.

Liam Ostlere (11)
Springfield Primary School, Linlithgow

Fun

Fun is multicoloured like the rainbow,
It feels like flying in the sky, your imagination
Going wild and dancing on the clouds.
It smells like lavender and all the pretty flowers,
It tastes like sweets, chocolate and all my favourite food,
It looks like a child smiling ear to ear,
It reminds me of my family and friends all happy and cheerful.

Fiona McLean (11)
Springfield Primary School, Linlithgow

Sadness

Sadness is dark grey, like a cloud of thick black smoke,
It smells so strongly, like vomit, it makes you tremble,
It looks like an empty fireplace in a dull damp room,
It sounds like a feeble moan of a hungry child,
It feels like the cold air in a dark, damp cellar,
It reminds me of dark, dreary and lonely alleys,
It tastes like bitter, mouldy sickness.

Kirsten Hall (10)
Springfield Primary School, Linlithgow

Fear

Fear is black like the black sea at night.
It sounds like screaming as terrorists destroy the Twin Towers,
It tastes like bitterness and poison,
It smells like body odour, after a tennis match,
It looks like a murderer's face with thunder and lightning
in the background,
It feels like hatred and ice and nothing but darkness,
It reminds me of dead people waking up and escaping
from their tombs.

Callum Henry (10)
Springfield Primary School, Linlithgow

Fun

Fun is yellow like the sunshine sparkling in the sky,
It sounds like kids laughing and playing,
It tastes like sweet melting in your mouth,
It smells like flowers, smells so sweet,
It looks like cheerful people having fun,
It feels like silk, soft, smooth and great,
It reminds me of playing with my friends.

Karine Stalker (11)
Springfield Primary School, Linlithgow

Darkness

Darkness is as black as smoke coming from Hell,
It feels like children crying in the night,
It sounds like a devil laughing on your back,
It smells like some people drinking and smoking in the park,
It looks like space with all the lights as stars,
It tastes like a cake which has been for days in an oven,
It reminds me of people going to sleep.

Grant Andrew Maclean (11)
Springfield Primary School, Linlithgow

Darkness

It's as black as cats wandering through dark tunnels,
It tastes like dark shadowed spells melting on your tongue,
It sounds like children screaming for help, as the bogeyman
has struck.

It feels like ghosts running through your soul one by one,
It smells like dark and daring secrets never told,
It reminds me of cold dark nights that I never slept through.

Corrie Hyslop (11)
Springfield Primary School, Linlithgow

Fear

Fear is as bright pinky-blue as a clear night sky at sunset,
It tastes like the sourness of poisoned blood,
It sounds like the running and screaming when air raid sirens sound,
It looks like the forked lightning in a pitch-black sky,
It smells like the odour from a sewer's pipe,
It feels like a burning coal in the palm of your hand.
It reminds me of the face of a murderer with flaming eyes.

Graeme Poole (11)
Springfield Primary School, Linlithgow

Fun

Fun is yellow like a happy smiling sun,
It tastes like ice cream melting in your mouth
on a hot summer's day,
It looks like people enjoying themselves
having the time of their lives,
It reminds me of all the happy times I had
with my gran before she died,
It sounds like children laughing,
It feels like happiness filling up your heart,
It smells like sweets and flowers, nice things
that you like.

Sarah McDonald (11)
Springfield Primary School, Linlithgow

Ánger

Anger is black like the midnight sky,
It smells like burning bodies fading away in the graveyard,
It tastes like mud mixed in a cauldron,
It sounds like the screaming voices in my head,
It looks like the black hole of death,
It feels like fire surrounding me,
It reminds me of a graveyard filled with unhappy souls.

Allison Macdonald (11)
Springfield Primary School, Linlithgow

Sadness

Sadness is blue like a cold, freezing, dark night,
It sounds like the wind howling at the grey clouds,
It feels like snow stuffed in your jacket pocket,
It reminds me of a stray cat purring for food,
It tastes of frozen peas that have been in the freezer for years,
It smells of cold air stuck in your nose,
It looks like poor people who are starving to death.

Lucy Pilcher (11)
Springfield Primary School, Linlithgow

Happiness

Happiness is yellow like the bright summer sun,
It smells like honey fresh from a beehive,
It sounds like birds singing in the trees,
It reminds me of a puppy wagging its tail,
It tastes like petals from a flower swaying in a meadow,
It looks like a pony running free in a grassy field,
It feels like a baby rabbit with its soft fur.

Eilidh McCall (10)
Springfield Primary School, Linlithgow

Happiness

Happiness is multicoloured like children playing in the park,
It sounds like a bluebird humming,
It tastes like a mouth-watering piece of chocolate gateau,
It looks like blossoms blooming on trees,
It smells like ripe strawberries,
It feels like Skips melting in my mouth,
It reminds me of the good times I have playing with my friends.

Catriona Haig (10)
Springfield Primary School, Linlithgow

Happiness

Happiness is bright like the sunny blue sky,
Happiness tastes like refreshing tasty juice,
Happiness smells like fresh washing,
Happiness looks like a bright cheerful face,
Happiness feels like I haven't done anything wrong,
It reminds me of getting everything right.

Neil Scullion (11)
Springfield Primary School, Linlithgow

Hunger

Hunger is clear like water in a glass,
It sounds like the rumbling of Niagara Falls in Canada,
It tastes like plastic with no taste at all,
It smells like a glorious feast torturing you all the more,
It looks like a never-ending hole, empty and plain,
It feels like an itch on your back that you can't reach,
It reminds me of the people in Sudan who suffer night and day.

Michael Boyle (11)
Springfield Primary School, Linlithgow

Fun!

Fun is violet like the sunset in the evening,
It tastes like the first summer sun,
It sounds like the last whistle of the winter wind,
It smells like candyfloss just freshly made,
It looks like a newly born puppy yelping in the sunset,
It feels like the feeling when you are doing something really good,
It reminds me of a picnic on a glorious day in a wonderful park.

Rebecca Aitken (11)
Springfield Primary School, Linlithgow

Hate

Hate is black like the Devil's heart of stone,
It sounds like flames crackling inside of me waiting to come out,
It tastes like ashes burning on my tongue,
It smells like coal on a fire melting metals in the deadly World War II,
It looks like a werewolf calling to the moon, about to kill,
It feels like a sword stabbing me in the heart, and it will never heal,
It reminds me of having no friends, knowing that you are going
to be alone forever,
And that is why hatred is a very powerful weapon that should
not be unleashed.

Callum Alexander Small (11)
Springfield Primary School, Linlithgow

Love

Love is purely pink like a tulip in spring,
It reminds me of a mother and a cute little baby,
It smells like a bunch of dried lavender,
It sounds like a happy baby's laugh,
It feels like the fur of a small baby rabbit,
It looks like two kittens playing with a ball of wool,
It tastes like fresh water from the mountains.

Shona Lawson (11)
Springfield Primary School, Linlithgow

Silence

Silence is grey like the dark clouds on a rainy day,
It reminds me of sleeping knowing nothing of what is happening,
It sounds like the wind whistling through cracked windows,
It tastes like water - no taste at all,
It feels rough and hard like the bark of a tree,
It looks like a long, dark, winding tunnel,
It smells like the musty smell of rotten leaves and bark.

Adam Sorbie (11)
Springfield Primary School, Linlithgow

Fun

Fun is yellow and orange like the shining sun,
It sounds like me and my sisters laughing at the beach,
It looks like children playing in the park,
It tastes like chocolate melting in my mouth,
It smells like a beautiful rose in my garden,
It reminds me of my really good friends,
It feels like my auntie and uncle's dog's puppies.

Nicola Riddell (10)
Springfield Primary School, Linlithgow

Silence

Silence is golden like a new pound coin,
It feels like gold, melting in your hands,
It smells like freshly made bread coming out of an oven,
It sounds like floating on clear calm water, on an inflatable lilo,
It looks like a bright sunny afternoon,
It tastes like melted milk chocolate,
It looks like a morning, the sky going orange,
It reminds me of a farm, early in the morning, when everyone
is just waking up.

Lesley Wilson (11)
Springfield Primary School, Linlithgow

Fear

Is as black as an endless space,
It sounds like a scream from a dead person's face,
It looks like a timber wolf eating your body,
It feels like a fire devouring your courage,
It smells like a pot of very old porridge,
It reminds me of the blood flowing out of a bullet hole in a body,
It tastes like unripe blackcurrants, bitter and sour.

Conall Black (11)
Springfield Primary School, Linlithgow

Darkness

Darkness is black like a dark night about to explode,
It looks like it will go on and on and never stop in the cold damp night.
It tastes like a rush of air coming right from the Arctic,
It sounds like children screaming on their own, never to be found,
It smells like a pile of rotting bodies in a graveyard,
It feels like you're in a room that you can't escape from,
It reminds me of a scary black cat's eye staring right at me.

Chloé Milligan (10)
Springfield Primary School, Linlithgow

Silence

Silence is grey, emotionless, like a pale face,
It feels like the rough metal bars of a dark cage,
It looks like a wisp of cloud from the heavens,
It tastes like the pureness and freshness of the clear blue sky,
It smells like the salty water of the Black Sea,
It sounds like the gentle breeze of the winds of Venus,
It reminds me of an echo in an enclosed cave,
Enveloped in darkness.

Douglas Watt (10)
Springfield Primary School, Linlithgow

Darkness

Darkness is black like the bombs getting dropped,
It smells like ashes coming from an eruption of a volcano,
It tastes like the dark blood coming from a man's heart,
It sounds like a black rumble coming from the dark,
It feels like a flame that I'm holding in my hand,
It looks like the tip of a gun which has just been shot,
It reminds me of my Uncle Bill's death.

David Joseph McKay (10)
Springfield Primary School, Linlithgow

Darkness

Darkness is the colour black,
It sounds like the werewolves howling and calling,
It tastes like burnt ashes from a cigarette,
It smells like blood and fear,
It looks like bats from the dead,
It feels like zombies rising from their graves,
It reminds me of the clear midnight sky all black
    with a full bright moon and some shiny, glittery stars.

Simrat Panesar (11)
Springfield Primary School, Linlithgow

Sadness

Sadness is blue like crying tears,
It sounds like a river flowing with fears,
It reminds me of people frowning like lions,
It looks like rags from long, long ago,
It tastes like salt lying in your mouth,
It feels like paper being ripped apart,
It smells like the leaves of a conifer tree.

Clare Gillies (11)
Springfield Primary School, Linlithgow

Darkness

Darkness is as black as rats, when they're squeaking,
It smells like oil at a petrol station pump,
It looks like a dark forest at night,
It feels like being crushed and not being able to breathe,
It tastes like cod liver oil,
It sounds like eerie silence,
It reminds me of death and destruction.

Lorn Henderson (10)
Springfield Primary School, Linlithgow

Love

Love is red like roses,
Love feels like romance passing by,
Love tastes like happiness and loving care,
Love reminds me of when my aunt and uncle got married,
Love looks like people falling in love,
Love smells like roses,
Love sounds like a new baby gurgling.

Kim-Louise McGregor (10)
Springfield Primary School, Linlithgow

Fear

Fear is black like spiders' legs that are all hairy,
It feels like a shiver that goes right down your spine,
It reminds me of a funeral,
It sounds like a big storm coming,
It smells like the Black Death,
It tastes like a burnt pizza,
It looks like a big black cloud that comes down on your head.

Melissa Black (11)
Springfield Primary School, Linlithgow

Hate

Hate is red like blood,
It tastes like a bitter lemon,
It feels like a snake wrapping round me,
It reminds me of burning fire,
It sounds like screaming in my head,
It smells like a decaying corpse,
It looks like a torture room in my head.

James Mair (10)
Springfield Primary School, Linlithgow

Sadness

Sadness is navy blue like the deep dark ocean,
It feels like someone is pulling me down and down,
It tastes like a lump in my throat,
It sounds like people dying in World War II,
It smells like rotten cheese,
It reminds me of my cat miaowing its last miaow.

Jamie Coyle (11)
Springfield Primary School, Linlithgow

Darkness

Darkness is black like a raging storm thundering through the night,
It tastes like Coca-Cola flowing down my throat,
It sounds like silence echoing through my head,
It smells like sickly cocoa powder tickling the back of my throat,
It feels like fire burning through my body,
It looks like darkness ripping through the night,
It reminds me of when my nana died.

Jill Stanners (11)
Springfield Primary School, Linlithgow

Happiness

Happiness is light blue like the sky,
It tastes of pizza, nice and warm inside when you bite into it,
It sounds like nice things, birds in a tree,
It reminds me of being in bed and it's nice and warm,
It looks like birds flying in the blue sky with a breeze,
It feels like a gentle breeze,
It smells of fresh air running through me.

Neil Morrison (11)
Springfield Primary School, Linlithgow

Fun

Fun is yellow like the sun,
It feels like I'm warm and fuzzy inside,
It tastes like chocolate mint ice cream,
It sounds like laughter of children playing outside,
It reminds me of my little hamster,
It smells like flowers in the sun,
It looks like the bright golden Heaven.

Monique Elizabeth Yntema (10)
Springfield Primary School, Linlithgow

Laughter

Laughter is colourless,
It can be nasty or nice
It can represent darkness
Or it can represent light.
Through darkness, it feels full of sorrow.
It could tear down an empire and replace it tomorrow
While through light, it could rebuild it all
And keep on adding, no matter how tall.

Campbell Thomson (11)
Springfield Primary School, Linlithgow

Happiness

Happiness is blue like the lovely summer sky,
It sounds like the laughing of people,
It reminds me of when I went on holiday, happy and excited,
It looks like a dove gliding peacefully in the sky,
It smells like flowers and fruit,
It tastes like chocolate and lovely strawberries with cream,
It makes me feel happy and warm.

Julia Herd (11)
Springfield Primary School, Linlithgow

Laughter

Laughter is orange, like the sun,
Laughter smells like the seaside,
Laughter tastes like ice cream straight from the van,
Laughter sounds like children playing in the park,
Laughter feels like the softness of a cat,
Laughter looks like the circus,
Laughter reminds me of being tickled,
Laughter is fun.

Robyn Brown (11)
Springfield Primary School, Linlithgow

Hate

Hate is red like bright red blood,
It smells like a very strong smell,
It looks like death,
It feels like a sharp pain running through you,
like someone is torturing you,
It reminds me of having a really bad day,
It sounds like really horrible, loud, classical music,
It tastes like burning hot water.

Sam Parlett (11)
Springfield Primary School, Linlithgow

Happiness

Happiness is yellow like the sun in the sky,
Happiness sounds like a gentle tune,
Happiness tastes like lovely juicy strawberries,
Happiness looks like everyone smiling,
Happiness smells like birthday candles alight,
Happiness feels soft and gentle,
Happiness reminds me of when I am on holiday.

Emma Whitehead (11)
Springfield Primary School, Linlithgow

Silence

Silence is white, like paper waiting to be written on,
It reminds me of undiscovered castles waiting to be found,
It tastes like the sea air melting on my tongue,
It sounds like a pin dropping on a table, making a little clink as it lands,
It smells like lavender wafting to my nose,
It looks like a big cage that all the noise is locked up in and
can't get out.
Silence feels like all the sadness in the world has been washed away
And now it's nice and peaceful.

Mahri Nicholson (10)
Springfield Primary School, Linlithgow

Love

Love is pink like a flamingo in the zoo.
Love reminds me of people kissing,
Love tastes like chocolate with strawberries inside it,
Love sounds like a newborn baby crying,
Love smells like perfume on the wrist of a bride,
Love feels like silk on a dress,
Love looks like a new baby boy.

Allyn Preece (10)
Springfield Primary School, Linlithgow

Laughter

Laughter is yellow like sunflowers' tall, big stems that wave in the wind.
It feels like happiness that hits my body,
It reminds me of happy times I had in the past,
It looks like people are having fun,
It tastes like sweets in your mouth waiting to be sucked,
It sounds like the buzzing of bees in the sweet warm air,
It smells like primroses when they open their petals.

Lucy Nisbet (11)
Springfield Primary School, Linlithgow

Anger

Anger is like a boiling volcano with lava coming down, the colour of
boiling orange.
Anger feels like lava sticking me to the ground,
Anger sounds like a scream that won't come out,
Anger tastes like burning tar oozing down my throat,
Anger reminds me of death, while watching your loved one die
through glass and suddenly the heart monitor's beeping and people
come running, trying to keep them but there's nothing you can do
and the anger is boiling inside you.
Anger looks like sick in a bucket, rotting away all mouldy and smelly,
Anger smells like tar rotting in a junkyard.

Rebecca Sorrie (10)
Springfield Primary School, Linlithgow

Lossiemouth

L ighthouse shining over the caravan park,
O n the rainy nights it was hard to get to sleep.
S taying awake because of the rain hitting the roof,
S eagulls flying about every morning looking for food.
I mages of the cliffs I could see walking along the beach.
E very day I saw a lot of jets.
M any people walking around the caravan site,
O ver my head I could see a lovely blue sky.
U nder the ground, rabbits who always jumped up,
T o see all of these things in just one week was great.
H ome at last and I get to see my friends again.

Craig Smith (10)
Strathburn School, Inverurie

Inverurie

I n Brandsbutt
N ever wet which was good
V ery sunny sometimes
E very day was nice
R unning traffic going by every day
U would love it too
R eally fun at parks
I loved it because it was fun
E veryone thought it was fun.

David Robertson (10)
Strathburn School, Inverurie

England

E verywhere I went, it rained,
N ever was it sunny.
G ood swimming pool,
L ived in a chalet.
A nd hired bicycles.
N ever had tea out, always bought it.
D ad's always played golf.

    Centre Parcs in England.

Ross Napier (10)
Strathburn School, Inverurie

Niomi

N ever late for school
I nterested in reading
O ptimistic about school
M y favourite subject is storywriting
I maginative in art.

Niomi Murison (10)
Strathburn School, Inverurie

Snow

Sludgy and freezing
Never ever warm
Only comes in winter
When will it ever go?

Slipping through my fingers
And sneaking through my toes
Never in the city
Dad, do we have to go home?

When I turn the tap on, water sprinkles out
At the beach
The water is everywhere
Even in my juice
It's even in my water gun.

Dean Morris (9)
Strathburn School, Inverurie

My Mum - Haikus

Always cleaning up
I owe her so much, I do
I do love my mum.

Every day I live
She helps me with everything
Even when I'm bad

So I want to thank
Her for everything she's done
I do love my mum.

Molly Munro (10)
Strathburn School, Inverurie

Katie

K ind and caring
A ngel while sleeping
T rouble when awake
I s willing to help everybody
E ver ready to help.

Katie Mackenzie (10)
Strathburn School, Inverurie

Barbados

B ack in Scotland, rain, rain, rain,
A t Manchester airport, rain, rain, rain.
R ight at the moment we got off the plane
B arbados was so, so hot
A t the pool side, diving in the pool.
D on't push me in mum, no!
O uch! I think I've had enough
S almonella was horrid.

Alice Rose McInulty (9)
Strathburn School, Inverurie

Leaves

When leaves fall off the trees,
Scrunch, scrunch, scrunch!
I make them into one big pile,
Crunch, crunch, crunch!
When I am done, I jump,
Rumble, rumble, rumble!

Stefan Innes (9)
Strathburn School, Inverurie

Lauren

L oves playing with animals,
A nd reading books as well.
U nder all others, going to school!
R eady every morning
E specially on weekdays,
N ever ever late and usually not in trouble.

Lauren Gray (10)
Strathburn School, Inverurie

Washing Machines

Twirling, swirling, sloshing around,
I watch my trousers go round and round,
You were made to astound.
Cleaning my socks and pants and tops,
Twirling, swirling, sloshing around
You were made to astound.

Emily Florence (10)
Strathburn School, Inverurie

My Favourite Acrostic Poem
From Those I've Written!

A lot of buildings
B eside the sea, under the sun,
E ngineering going on.
R aging people, up and down.
D azzling lights at night.
E normous boats passing by.
E nough food for all.
N ever bored at night.

Callum Drysdale (10)
Strathburn School, Inverurie

Grant

G oes to Strathburn Primary School
R uns about at break time
A lways polite to teachers
N eat and tidy work he does
T o hand into the teacher.

Grant Dryburgh (10)
Strathburn School, Inverurie

Tiger - Haikus

Tigers are gorgeous
Prowling in the Savannah
Never saying words

They are very proud
Never scavenge for their food
Always first to strike

They are in danger
Their eyes are round, deep with fear
Poachers out at night.

Emma Donaldson (9)
Strathburn School, Inverurie

Nairn

N airn is wet and cold
A rgh! The sea has wet my toes,
I 'm now gathering shells,
R otten seaside smell,
N ow I'm building a sandcastle.

Rory Angus (10)
Strathburn School, Inverurie

Spain

S ummer sun all week long
P ity I had to leave
A nd next time I'll stay for two weeks
I n the six pools, all day long
N ever out, not even to eat.

Nicole Aitken (10)
Strathburn School, Inverurie

Pets

My favourite pet is a cat,
He is such a brat!
He is a fantastic acrobat,
But when he's in his bed
He acts like a piece of lead.

My cat loves to play
Along the great big bay.
He goes every single day
And has never lost his way.
Hurrah, hurrah for my pet cat!

Hannah Slater (10)
Stratherrick Primary School, Inverness

Bonny Loch Ness

One day by bonny Loch Ness
A tourist was playing chess
A monster jumped out
The tourist gave a great shout
And water splashed all over her dress.

Craig Hepburn (9)
Stratherrick Primary School, Inverness

The Pink Marshmallow Monster

The pink marshmallow monster
Has great big googly eyes.
He doesn't tell the truth
But tells astonishing lies.
He hides under bed covers
Until the children shout
'I'm not going in my room until
that monster's out!'
Every day he wanders, knocking on all the doors,
saying, 'If you let me stay I'll do all the chores!'
But this never works you see -
Because he's very, very ugly.
Plus he wouldn't fit at all
Because he's thirty-two feet tall.

Eleanor Parrott (10)
Stratherrick Primary School, Inverness

Pets

My favourite pet is a dog,
I have one at home.
My dog likes to carry a log
She also likes to chase rabbits.

I don't like cats
'Cause they scratch
And sleep on mats.

Rabbits could live in a hutch
And they like carrots.
They might be able to
Speak Dutch!

Little fish, just like
To live in dishes.
They are quite friendly
With jellyfish.

Lucy Fraser (10)
Stratherrick Primary School, Inverness

Anger

Anger sounds noisy and unpleasant,
Anger tastes bitter like red hot chilli peppers.
Anger smells like burning fire and smoke.
Anger looks like a black dragon with red eyes
And a red hissing snake.
Anger feels a lot like a fiery, tense lion.

Iseabail Parrott (7)
Stratherrick Primary School, Inverness

The Cat That Went Splat

There once was a very fat cat
who loved to eat birds and rats.
She ate all day and never wanted to play
and one day she burst with a splat!

Hannah Tweedlie (9)
Stratherrick Primary School, Inverness

Run

There was an old man from Ben
He had nothing but an old hen
When he tried to kill it
It turned round with a rocket kit
His aim was incredibly bad
He shot the rocket
It flew like a jet
And killed his little pet.

Ruairidh Fraser (11)
Stratherrick Primary School, Inverness

Fun

Fun sounds like children on a bouncy castle
and an egg and spoon race.
Fun tastes like melted chocolate and
chocolate crispies.
Fun smells like roses in a vase and
freshly baked buns.
Fun looks like going on a trampoline
and coming down a slide.
Fun feels like standing in the rain
under an umbrella and paddling
at the beach.

Emma Fraser (8)
Stratherrick Primary School, Inverness

I Hate School

I see the school in my dream
It smells and tastes like lumpy cream!
Even when I'm home at night
The thought of school gives me a fright!
As I wake up in my bed, I think of what
I really dread!
The sound of my alarm, I hate
And the shutting of the garden gate.
As I'm walking to the bus
I think of all the noise and fuss,
The only good thing is my mate
All school makes me think is *hate.*

Kyle Easter (11)
Stratherrick Primary School, Inverness

Hallowe'en

There once was a witch
Who had an itch
Her name was Titch
And her cat was called Stitch

There once was a ghost
Who lived by the coast
He loved to eat toast
And liked to boast

There once was a cat
Who was very fat
He had a pet rat
And wore a witch's hat

There once was a wizard
Who got caught in a blizzard
His spell went wrong
And now he's a lizard

On October 31st
Go out if you must
But watch out for a fuss
If you see the witch, the ghost -
The cat or the wizard.

Matthew Ricketts (9)
Stratherrick Primary School, Inverness

Summer

Summer sounds like singing birds,
Summer tastes like candyfloss.
Summer smells like fresh cut grass,
Summer looks like bees flying from flower to flower
Summer feels like hot air rushing towards me.

Fraser MacLennan (11)
Stratherrick Primary School, Inverness

My Dog

I like my dog
Although he drinks from the bog
When he goes out at night
The fox in the garden gives him a fright
When he goes to bed
He expects to be fed
When he sees a rat
He acts like a prat
And he loves to play with a cricket bat.

Harry Stoppard (11)
Stratherrick Primary School, Inverness

Animalz

I saw a cow in a field
who came out with a sword and a shield.
He went to war
and came back with a bee and a boar.
After that, he jumped about
and ate a sprout.
He got in a car and played his guitar
and went to sleep to a pop star.

Jak Bryant (10)
Stratherrick Primary School, Inverness

Chip

There once was a horse called Chip
Who was very naughty and liked to nip.

But he was very good at his trot and
All the mares thought he was hot.

Annie Butterworth (10)
Stratherrick Primary School, Inverness

Fun

Fun sounds like children laughing in the playground
and birds chirping in the trees.

Fun tastes sweet like chocolate or ice cream
on a hot sunny day.

Fun smells like the bakery or a bubble bath
with fairy jasmine bath bombs.

Fun looks like pretty butterflies and
cute teddy bears.

Fun feels like a warm shower after a cool swim
or your tummy, when you drive over a bump in the road.

Melissa Cumming (7)
Stratherrick Primary School, Inverness

Happiness

Happiness sounds like the waves on the shore
Or the ice cream van, as it stops at my door.

Happiness tastes like egg mayonnaise
Or mint ice cream on hot, sunny days.

Happiness smells like a freshly made scone
Or grass left behind on a newly mown lawn.

Happiness looks like my dog at the gate
Or when I open the door and see my mate.

Happiness feels like my old, raggy teddy
Or when Mum shouts, 'Tea's ready!'

Ewen Fraser (9)
Stratherrick Primary School, Inverness

Spring

Spring feels like a new life,
It reminds me of when I was born
Spring feels like a water pipe has expanded
It reminds me of floods in countries

Spring is the time when colours come to Earth
The flowers are as yellow as the sun
The sky is as blue as the sea
The clouds are as white as snow.

Spring looks like Heaven
I see lots of fruits growing
I see lots of baby animals
Spring looks like my friend.

I can hear birds chirping
I can hear dogs barking
I can hear the wind whistling
I can hear crying babies.

Jack Harrison (9)
Townhead Primary School, Coatbridge

Spring

Spring feels like I am melting in the sun
It reminds me of a holiday
Spring feels nice and cool
It reminds me of winter

I can hear a train going past
A train going to Glasgow
To see my granda
Because I love my granda.

Spring is as green as grass
It reminds me of my toys
Spring is as yellow as the sun
Spring is as red as roses.

Joseph Brannigan (10)
Townhead Primary School, Coatbridge

Winter

Winter feels like an ice cube
It reminds me of an ice berg
Winter is like an ice sculpture
It reminds me of an ice cave.

Winter is as white as the Antarctic
Winter is like a white angel
Winter is full of white snow
I like to throw snowballs
At my friends.

I saw snowmen in the gardens
I saw birds taking shelter in the trees
I saw that the trees were covered in snow
I saw children making slides.

I heard owls hooting
I heard the wind blowing
I heard the snow hitting the windows
I heard people talking in the dark.

Mark Plunkett (9)
Townhead Primary School, Coatbridge

Summer

Summer feels like a generator,
It reminds me of Menorca.
Summer feels like a fire,
It reminds me of lava.

Summer is as red as Mars,
It reminds me of space.
Summer is as gold as the sun,
It reminds me of gold coins.

Summer looks like the ground is burning,
It reminds me of meteors,
Summer looks like you can cook in it
It reminds me of curry.

In summer I can hear birds singing,
It reminds me of dogs barking,
In summer I can hear lawnmowers
It reminds me of cats purring.

Aaron Johnstone (9)
Townhead Primary School, Coatbridge

Spring

Spring is as red as lava
It reminds me of Spain
Spring feels like a hot air balloon
It reminds me of Salou

Spring is as sunny as the sun
It reminds me of Mexico City
It is the best time on Earth
It reminds me of the Caribbean

I hear the dogs barking in the background
It reminds me of Cyprus
I hear the sheep in the background
It reminds me of Egypt.

I can hear the birds chirping
It reminds me of people whistling
I can hear the horses coming up the road
It reminds me of fireworks.

Robert Gardner (8)
Townhead Primary School, Coatbridge

Spring

Spring feels like a fresh new start
It reminds me of a cool place in Greece
Spring feels like it's going to be a big bang
It reminds me of fireworks.

Spring is as red as lava
It reminds me when the men put red stuff in the pool
Spring is as white as the clouds
It reminds me of when I jumped off a cliff.

Spring looks bright
It reminds me of the bright sky
Spring looks like yellow
It reminds of the yellow sun.

I can hear the birds singing
They reminds me of the singing donkey
I can hear the birds shouting
They remind me that me and my friends were shouting.

Denise Taylor (8)
Townhead Primary School, Coatbridge

Winter

Winter feels like a freezer
It reminds me of the Atlantic,
Winter feels like an ice sculpture
It reminds me of Iceland.

Winter is as white as snow
It reminds me of Alaska,
Winter is as blue as the sea
It reminds me of Christmas.

Winter looks like an icicle
It reminds me of snow,
Winter looks like a snowman
It reminds me of the sea.

In winter I can hear the wind,
It reminds me of Snow White,
In winter I can hear gates banging
It reminds me of doors slamming.

Miguel Barroso (8)
Townhead Primary School, Coatbridge

Spring

Spring feels like flying
It reminds me of planes
Spring feels like jumping
It reminds me of my pogo stick.

I can hear the cows grazing
It reminds me of the park,
I can hear sheep
It reminds me of my sister.

Spring is as yellow as butter
It reminds me of giraffes,
Spring is as green as grass
It reminds me of trees.

Spring looks like a bunch of flowers
It reminds me of roses,
Spring looks like a pile of lambs
It reminds me of daisies.

Shona MacLean (9)
Townhead Primary School, Coatbridge

Summer

Summer feels like an oven
It reminds me of being at the beach,
Summer feels like a fire
It reminds me of the sun.

Summer is as red as a rose
It reminds me of a ball of fire,
Summer is as red as Mars
It reminds me of being on holiday.

Summer looks like the sun
It reminds me of a flame,
Summer looks like a fire
It reminds me of an explosion of fire.

In the summer I can hear people playing
It reminds me of being on holiday
In the summer I can hear birds chirping
It reminds me of spring.

Aiden Owen (9)
Townhead Primary School, Coatbridge

Winter

Winter feels like a giant snowman
It reminds me of Snow White,
Winter feels like the Atlantic Ocean,
It reminds me of Iceland.

Winter is as white as the clouds
It reminds me of a freezing refrigerator,
Winter looks like white cats
It reminds me of cold chalk.

Winter looks like white clouds
It reminds me of snow,
Winter looks like snowy mountains
It reminds me of a snowy pond.

I can hear the wind outside my window
I can hear the branches of the trees,
I can hear snow crunching under my feet
I can hear rain splashing on the ground.

Russell Chalmers (9)
Townhead Primary School, Coatbridge

The Seasons

Summer feels like the day I went to the show
It reminds me of the day I was on holiday,
Summer feels like the pretty days
It reminds me of day I went ice skating.

Winter feels as cool as ice
It reminds me of the day I was born,
Winter feels like snow on the grass
It reminds me of my mum telling me about the winter.

Autumn feels like when flowers come out of the grass
It reminds me of the day I saw rabbits hopping,
Autumn feels like jumping in the leaves
It reminds me of being on my pogo stick.

Spring feels cool, hot and happy
It reminds me of happy times,
Spring feels like a cool breeze
It reminds me of the day my mum got me a chain.

Natasha McKinley
Townhead Primary School, Coatbridge